"The way of wisdom is the way of Chr[i]
Christ cannot be compartmentalized
the whole of life both when we are a[t]
and Greeson understand this, and they help us see the Christ
way with biblical fidelity and clarity. I gladly commend this
book to all who long to think Christianly in their context and
live the same."

—**Daniel L. Akin**, president, Southeastern
Baptist Theological Seminary

"This is a little book, but only in size. Its beautiful style and
accessibility rightly conceal the wealth of thought and analysis
underlying it. I wish that as a teenage Christian in apartheid
South Africa I'd had something like this: a framework for understanding culture and Christian engagement with it. The issues
addressed in this book not only connect us with the hidden
glory of mundane things, like changing diapers and riding bi-
cycles, but provide a framework for understanding our involve-
ment in culture—all beautifully centered around the metaphor
of walking. If the American church, particularly in the West, is
to bear witness to Christ and to enhance his reputation, then it
must address these questions. Only in this way will we avoid the
idolatries that swirl around our cultures. Quinn and Greeson are
excellent guides through this discussion and point the reader
toward additional sources for further exploration."

—**Craig G. Bartholomew**, director of the Kirby
Laing Centre for Public Theology, Cambridge, UK

"Contemporary Christians are asking what it means to faithfully steward their place in this moment. Competing models
and frameworks vie for our attention and adaptation. Benjamin
Quinn and Dennis Greeson present a compelling vision by root-
ing our engagement in the larger story of what God is doing in the
world. For those looking beyond cheap slogans and temporary

fixes, *The Way of Christ in the Culture* offers a durable political theology for twenty-first-century believers. This is not just a resource for pastors and scholars, but a helpful guide for believers in every vocation."

—**Daniel Darling**, director of the Land Center for Cultural
Engagement, Southwestern Baptist Theological Seminary

"Quinn and Greeson's *The Way of Christ in Culture* is not just a wonderful introduction to the Christian's relationship to culture; it is a compelling vision for how we should live our lives in every detail. Drawing on the rich tradition of the Dutch Reformed and the wisdom of Proverbs, the authors help us see how God's intent for our lives touches literally everything we do in the world. This is exactly the kind of book I want my students to read, and Quinn and Greeson are exactly the people I'd want to write it!"

—**Jamie Dew**, president, New Orleans
Baptist Theological Seminary

"In this beautifully written and thoughtfully organized volume, Benjamin Quinn and Dennis Greeson have provided illuminating and thoughtful counsel for Christ followers who desire to walk faithfully and wisely with God in all aspects of life. Offering biblical, theological, historical, and contemporary framing, *The Way of Christ in Culture* calls on readers to reflect deeply on God's call for his people to think and live Christianly in order to engage culture for the glory of God. The work of Quinn and Greeson is everyday theology at its best, helping all of us to make known God's way on the earth and his salvation among the nations. I am delighted to recommend this fine work and look forward to forthcoming volumes in this series."

—**David S. Dockery**, president, Southwestern
Baptist Theological Seminary

"Drawing from the riches of the Reformed tradition, *The Way of Christ in Culture* offers a wonderful introduction to what it means to see our everyday, ordinary lives as places to seek Christ and follow him. Not only will readers find a clear and insightful exploration of culture from within the biblical story, but they will also be equipped to engage in thoughtful reflection on what it means to be cultural creatures whose aim is to behold Christ in and through our lives."

—**Gayle Doornbos**, associate professor
of theology, Dordt University

"In every time and in every place, Christians wrestle with how to navigate their culture faithfully. For believers in an increasingly post-Christian West, this issue looms especially large. We need wise guides. Drawing on insights from the Kuyperian tradition, Benjamin Quinn and Dennis Greeson offer a path to flourishing in a culture prone to revolt against its heritage."

—**Nathan A. Finn**, Institute for Transformational
Leadership, North Greenville University

"The authors of this work are convinced that the way of the Lord is the way of life. Not just the way to life in the world to come, but real, God-given life now on our pilgrimage to endless and perfect life. The beautiful clarity of this book is rooted in deep reflection on both Scripture and wise voices in the history of the church. There is so much here about being human that is enriching and satisfying. I hope you will enjoy this for yourself as you seek to be wise in the culture that the Lord has placed you in to shape."

—**Michael McClenahan**, principal and professor
of systematic theology, Union Theological
College, Belfast, Northern Ireland

"I have long worried that in focusing on 'high' and 'popular' culture, our studies of 'Christ and culture' leave a whole range of cultural activity out of the picture. Not this wonderful book. I knew that the authors were serious about following the way of cultural obedience in all of creation when I read this savvy declaration in the first chapter: 'Changing a diaper, though seemingly mundane, is a magnificent act of culture.'"

—**Richard J. Mouw**, president emeritus,
Fuller Theological Seminary

"In *The Way of Christ in Culture*, Quinn and Greeson give us a wonderful primer on cultural engagement. The book situates our lives in God's story, and, through the synthesis of biblical, theological, and historical sources, it casts a vision for walking in the way of Christ in the world. This calling challenges people of faith to embrace a renewed purpose and vocation: to walk wisely in the world. This involves asking the right kinds of questions that will guide us toward living culturally embedded lives that shape the world around us in new and beautiful ways. Readers will be inspired to walk the way of Christ, which is a cultural path that leads to the kingdom of God."

—**Stephen Presley**, senior fellow for religion and public
life, Center for Religion, Culture, and Democracy

"Greeson and Quinn ably and winsomely remind us that our way in the world as Christians is an old, ancient way, but one renewed for today by God himself. This old-but-renewed way has always been a command to live faithfully in particular times and places, meaning that Christ followers interact with culture and create culture. Whether it involves conversations about nature and grace, Niebuhr's categories, or Kuyper and Dutch Neo-Calvinism, this volume continually weaves back to wisdom and the path of Christ in a way that calls real followers to follow Jesus."

—**Jacob Shatzer**, associate provost and
dean of instruction, Union University

"A lovely little primer in what promises to be an edifying and exciting series. The call for us to walk in the way of the Lord in the whole of creation is precisely that: a calling, our calling. This volume orientates us, setting us in the right direction and setting us up for future exploration."

—**Dan Strange**, director, Crosslands Forum

"If culture is the 'ways and products of creatures in creation,' then thinking well about how to cultivate a culture in the way of Jesus is an inescapable Christian and creaturely responsibility. Quinn and Greeson have written an accessible primer on the relationship between Christ and culture, and this book invites us to consider the deep resources of Scripture and tradition for reflection on this perennial topic."

—**N. Gray Sutanto**, assistant professor of systematic theology, Reformed Theological Seminary

"Often, Christians see culture as merely something external to us that must be engaged rather than recognizing that it is much more complex and all-encompassing. Not only do we engage it, but we are part of it and shaped by it. In order to cultivate wisdom, Christians must slow down to ask the right questions about our world as we seek to frame all of life in light of the way of Christ. Quinn and Greeson provide a very helpful introduction to culture and Christian thought that will expose you to numerous thinkers and ideas on the relationship between Christ and culture as well as equip you to think biblically about the whole of the Christian life, rooted in the love of God and love of neighbor."

—**Jason Thacker**, assistant professor of philosophy and ethics, Boyce College and Southern Seminary

THE
Way
OF
Christ
IN
Culture

THE
Way
OF
Christ
IN
Culture

A Vision for All of Life

BENJAMIN T. QUINN &
DENNIS T. GREESON

ACADEMIC
BRENTWOOD, TENNESSEE

The Way of Christ in Culture: A Vision for All of Life
Copyright © 2024 by Benjamin T. Quinn and Dennis T. Greeson

Published by B&H Academic®
Brentwood, Tennessee

ISBN: 978-1-0877-7511-1

Dewey Decimal Classification: 261.1
Subject Heading: CULTURE CONFLICT \ CHRISTIAN SOCIOLOGY \
RELIGION AND SOCIOLOGY

The web addresses referenced in this book were live and correct at the time of the book's publication but may be subject to change.

Cover design by Emily Keafer Lambright. Cover images by torkile/iStock, Yaro75/iStock, phant/iStock, iralu/iStock.

Printed in the United States of America

29 28 27 26 25 24 VP 1 2 3 4 5 6 7 8 9 10

For B. A. and A. W.

CONTENTS

PREFACE

How happy are those whose way is blameless,
who walk according to the Lord's instruction! . . .
They do nothing wrong; they walk in his ways.
—Psalm 119:1, 3

Time and again the Bible uses the ordinary and familiar meta-phor of walking to describe our lives before God. Walking—not crawling, running, or flying—but faithful and steady walking in the ways of the Lord is our God-given instruction in the world. When we choose to walk another way, such as following the way of Lady Folly, as Proverbs illustrates so vividly (Proverbs 7 and 9 in particular), we learn that such a way ends in death and meaninglessness—"like chaff that the wind blows away" (Ps 1:4). The way of the Lord, however, is the way of life.

As God's imagers in the world, we are called to walk in his ways in every area of life. This way of living extends beyond the walls of our churches, theological schools, mission agen-cies, and prayer rooms. Like Lady Wisdom who calls out from the highest places in the town, we are to advance God's ways in the whole of his creation, in every time and place, and in every cultural sphere.

While few Christians would disagree with this calling, it seems that even fewer are prepared to offer a clear, biblical, and Christ-centered model for how to walk in this way. Books and resources abound regarding new methods in evangelism, daily Bible reading, improving prayer life, and tips for Christian parents. For each of these, I am deeply grateful.

But what about the rest of life? What does it look like to "walk in the way of the Lord" in the whole of creation?

The Christ in Everything series demonstrates how Christ is connected to all of life, offering a vision for how to advance the way of Christ in all of life. From citizenship and political matters to science, the nature of truth, human embodiment, technology, sexuality, sports, and more, the Christ in Everything primers serve as introductions to important cultural topics by providing a biblical and theological framework from which to view and approach the topic at hand, followed by examples of how to walk in the way of Jesus in that cultural domain.

As with any book, these volumes are products of particular times and places. Further, they are written by Westerners embedded in Western contexts. This is neither a subtle preference for the West nor a slight toward the rest of the world. Rather, we seek to apply the transcending wisdom of Scripture to our particular times and places. Consequently, the nature of the conversations will change over time, and eventually these volumes will feel outdated. But while the cultural particulars will change, we hope the biblical and theological frameworks put forward in these volumes will transcend cultural trends and warrant a long shelf-life both in your library and in your heart.

Regardless of your vocation or station in life, we pray these volumes will help us all walk more faithfully and steadily in the way of Jesus.

Benjamin T. Quinn
Wake Forest, NC
May 2023

ACKNOWLEDGMENTS

We wish to thank the following for their contributions and support of this volume and the series as a whole:

B&H Academic—especially Madison Trammel and Michael McEwen for your willingness to contract and oversee such a series. Even when we struggled to articulate clear vision, you saw the need and opportunity.

Southeastern Baptist Theological Seminary and BibleMesh—to both organizations and their respective leadership, thank you for your unwavering support of our work!

Team Quinn and the Greeson family—our wives and children play indispensable roles in volumes like the present one. Endless conversations, brainstorming, and support of the times we are away at work . . . we can't thank you enough!

Dan Strange—for your review of the initial draft. Your careful read and constructive feedback made for a much better volume. Thank you!

For various editorial and administrative assistance, special thanks to Sam Bullington, Rachel Smith, Billie Goodenough, and Megan Dickerson.

1

The Way of Christ in the Biblical Story

Jesus is an alternative to the dominant ways
of the world, not a supplement to them.
—Eugene Peterson, *The Jesus Way:*
A Conversation on the Ways That Jesus Is the Way

When I was a toddler, my (Benjamin's) favorite book was *I Can Do It Myself*, featuring Jim Henson's *Sesame Street* Muppets. I do not recall much about this season of my life, but my parents love to remind me that not only was this my favorite book, but the title of the book was also my favorite phrase. I was fond of insisting, "I can do it myself!" Part of the terrible twos, no doubt. I wish I could tell you that I left this childish mindset in the toddler years, but sadly I did not. It followed me into adolescence, then the teen years, early adulthood, and now into whatever the forties is called. The truth is, I still like to insist, "I can do it myself!"

But what am I saying with this assertion? First is *the insistence of human autonomy* and the faulty assumption that "my way" is good, true, and beautiful. The deeper tones of this declaration are not simply "I can do it myself!" but the more dangerous "I will do it *my way!*"

"My way!" places self at the center of the world. It orients all things around my will, my wants, my desires, my preferences; it puts me first in line and glorifies me. It assumes that I know best, that I am first, and that everything and everyone would do well to organize their lives around me. It declares, "My kingdom come and my will be done on earth as it is in my heart." The problem is, God does not make room for "my way" in his kingdom.

The "My way!" story makes me the beginning, middle, and end of all things. It is a sad and hopeless story that no one should read. In Thomas Hobbes's fashion, this story is nasty, brutish, and short. It is not a way worth walking or worth living. The Bible tells a rather different story. It tells of the Creator God and his Son Jesus, the King of creation. This story—the *True Story of the Whole World*—tells us who this God is, what he has done, and the way that we—as His imagers—*ought* to live in his world.[1] It is a twisty-turvy story of a good God, a stubborn nation, a miracle-working Savior, and a renewed people called and empowered by God to advance the way of Christ in the world. This chapter seeks to tell that story, God's story, as *the starting place for understanding the way of Christ in culture.*

---

[1] A tip of the hat to Michael Goheen and Craig Bartholomew's excellent book, *The True Story of the Whole World: Finding Your Place in the Biblical Drama* (Grand Rapids: Brazos, 2020).

The Way in Creation

"In the beginning, God created the heavens and the earth" (Gen 1:1). Such is the first sentence of the Bible. This will doubtless be familiar to most, but let us reflect briefly on three parts of this sentence.

In the Beginning

We might read this as "First things first," suggesting that this is the most important piece of information to prepare you for this story. Without this, you cannot understand the rest. We might also read this as "the first act in time," meaning that nothing occurred in time and space as we know it prior to this event. These words establish the beginning of the timeline that we are still part of today.

Or we might also hear it in a more personal manner. "In the beginning" certainly signals something about the beginning of time, but it also signals something about *the One who is the beginning*. The apostle John took this cue at the beginning of his Gospel when he wrote, "In the beginning was the Word, and the Word was with God, and the Word was God. He was with God in the beginning" (John 1:1–2). Thus, to read Gen 1:1 as John read it, "In the beginning" doesn't merely identify the beginning of time. It identifies a person, the Word who was with God "in the beginning." And "in this beginning" God created.

God Created

It is worth noting that in the opening line of the Bible, we do not merely meet God. We meet God *at work*! This hardly bothers contemporary readers today, but the notion of a god working would have been blasphemous for most of the ancient world. The "good life" was assumed to be the life of leisure and rest, not work. And if the gods are exemplars of this life of leisure, work must certainly have been far from their line of duty.

But not the God of the Bible. In the same opening sentence, we are introduced to this Elohim (a generic Hebrew word for God) who created the heavens and the earth, and he did so "in the beginning." The story continues by informing us that the earth was formless, empty, and dark. Like a blank canvas awaiting the artist's imaginative brilliance. But before filling the canvas, we learn more about this God. He is Spirit. More to come on this point, but to recap the first two verses, God is "in the beginning"; he is creator of heaven and earth; he is Spirit; and, though the Creator, he is not *of* creation. And all the while, he is a worker.

The Heavens and the Earth

The paired "heavens and earth" captures everything that is. While the canvas remains blank, so to speak, "heavens and earth" indicate that the *structure* of all things (seen and unseen) was created by this "in the beginning" God. The Christian tradition has bequeathed to us the Latin phrase *creatio ex nihilo*, creation out of nothing, meaning that God did not use preexisting materials to construct the world. He simply spoke, and "out of nothing" came something—namely the heavens and earth and everything else that was made.

And it was made "in the beginning." This personal Word served as the tool of creation, the means through which all things came into being (Psa 33:6; John 1:1–3; Col 1:15–17;

Heb 1:1–2). Just as an artist leaves traces of his nature and character in his art, so too has the Creator crafted the *structure* and *direction* of the world in accord with his nature and character. God's *way* is woven into creation *through his beginning*— the Word—interlacing all things with all that is good, true, and beautiful as befits the character of God.[2] This underscores the fact that God is the author of culture. He is the first culture-maker, as will be discussed in greater detail in later chapters. We may especially highlight the biblical theme of wisdom here as Al Wolters, quoting James Fleming, stresses: "'Wisdom . . . was wrought into the constitution of the universe,' so that 'man's wisdom was to know this divine Wisdom—plan, order—and attune his ways to it.' Consequently, 'wisdom meant conforming to the divine constitution. One must find out what it is, then order himself accordingly.' In a word, 'wisdom is ethical conformity to God's creation.'"[3]

Interlude on Creation

Before continuing the story, we pause to underscore the terms *structure* and *direction*. As we will argue throughout, all of

---

[2] This is not to suggest that the very divine nature (*homoousious*) of the Godhead is embedded in the creation, rather that there is a recognizable reflection of the Creator in his creation, chiefly in human beings, that points toward his intended way in the world. As Oliver O'Donovan rightly asserts, "The way the universe *is*, determines how man *ought* to behave himself in it." *Resurrection and Moral Order: An Outline for Evangelical Ethics*, 2nd ed. (Grand Rapids: Eerdmans, 1994), 17.

[3] Al Wolters, *Creation Regained: Biblical Basics for a Reformational Worldview*, 2nd ed. (Grand Rapids: Eerdmans, 2005), 29.

creation is formed with both a basic *structure* and an intended *direction*. Structure speaks to the form and content, or the order, of a created thing, while direction speaks to its purpose and function as designed by God. Wolters writes, "*Structure* is anchored in the law of creation . . . It designates a reality that the philosophical tradition of the West has often referred to by such words as *substance, essence, and nature.*"[4]

Direction, Wolters adds, "designates the order of sin and redemption, the distortion or perversion of creation through the fall on the one hand and the redemption and restoration of creation in Christ on the other. Anything in creation can be directed either toward or away from God—that is, in obedience or disobedience to his law."[5] Human beings, for example, have a body-soul structure, and their direction is to believe and obey God. Jesus specifically refers to this as loving God with one's heart, soul, mind, and strength and loving one's neighbor as oneself. The "heart, soul, mind, and strength" speak to the structure of the person, while "loving" speaks to the direction (purpose) of the person.

When sin enters the story, it does not diminish the *structural* goodness of creation, but rather it seizes upon the *directional* nature of creation by introducing another way (a different order). The structure of the human being remains good as designed by God, but the direction of the human being (his or her way of life) is mis*directed*. This carries echoes of sin as that which "misses the mark" or, in Paul's imagery, "fall[s] short" of God's glory (Rom 3:23).

---

[4] Wolters, 59. Italics added.
[5] Wolters, 59.

As the story continues, by speaking his Word, God fills the earth with plants, animals, insects, birds, fish, and creatures of all kinds, complete with the potential to be fruitful and multiply. After six days and eight declarations of "Let it be!" from light to water to animals to people, God rested on the seventh day. After each day God beheld that what he had made was good. And because God rested on the seventh day, he blessed it and made it holy. As Cornelius Plantinga observed, "God doesn't talk all the time. God doesn't work all the time."[6] And we do well to imitate him in this.

God's Imagers—Male and Female

On the sixth day God made something particularly unique. After all the plants, birds, fish, livestock, and insects, God said, "Let us make man in our image, according to our likeness. They will rule the fish of the sea, the birds of the sky, the livestock, the whole earth, and the creatures that crawl on the earth" (Gen 1:26). And so he did. Verse 27 says, "So God created man in his own image; he created him in the image of God; he created them male and female."

God then blessed them and gave them the same instructions he had given the other creatures in v. 22 to be fruitful and multiply. But there was more. To his imagers God gave additional responsibility: "Fill the earth, and subdue it. Rule . . . every creature that crawls on the earth" (Gen 1:28). Genesis 2:15 summarizes this further by stating, "The LORD God took

---

[6] Cornelius Plantinga, *Engaging God's World: A Christian Vision of Faith, Learning, and Living* (Grand Rapids: Eerdmans, 2002), 29.

the man and placed him in the garden of Eden *to work it and watch over it"* (emphasis added).

For our purposes here, we will consider three insights from this passage. First, God's imagers—male and female—are the stewards of all creation. Unlike the plants, animals, fish, and flying creatures, Adam and Eve were uniquely created in God's image and likeness. While other creatures were instructed to be fruitful, multiply, and fill the earth in various ways, only those made in God's image were instructed to subdue the earth and have dominion over it, to work it and keep it.[7] This is a weighty responsibility.

Second, to subdue and exercise dominion implies *direction*, not domination. It is Adam and Eve's responsibility to recognize what ought to happen in God's world, then *direct* all things accordingly. They are to subdue enemies and threats and point all of creation, like rows in a garden, toward the way of the Creator. Working and keeping God's garden is about promoting and preserving. Promoting the way of the Creator while preserving its integrity. Promoting works toward filling the earth with God's abundance. Preserving speaks of keeping to the way of the Creator and subduing any threats to that way. All of this

---

[7] As several have pointed out, the verbs here "to work" and "to keep" have distinctly cultic or religious connotations. William Dumbrell explains, "The two verbs used in the account to depict Adam's role, 'cultivate' (*abad*) and 'guard' (*shamar*), are elsewhere in the OT translated when used singly for serving or guarding as priestly service in the tabernacle (Num. 3:7–8; 8:25–26; 18:5–6; 1 Chr. 23:32; Ezek. 44:14, cf. also Isa. 56:6). The only other time the OT uses both verbs together is in connection with the Levitical service and guarding of the sanctuary (Num. 3:7–8; 8:25–26)." William J. Dumbrell, *Creation and Covenant: An Old Testament Covenant Theology* (Milton Keynes, UK: Paternoster, 2013), 44.

speaks of proper dominion over creation. God's imagers are responsible to work and keep, promote and preserve, multiply and fill the earth, subdue and exercise dominion. This is still our responsibility as imagers of God.

The third insight is the link between imagers and culture. The task of promoting and preserving is the call to keep and cultivate the way of God in his world. This was our original vocation, our original purpose, and this is still our vocation and purpose despite the complication of sin.

Another Way?

Early in the biblical story, we learn that there is an alternative to God's will and way in the world. Following his instruction to Adam to "work and keep" the garden, God commands that Adam eat of every tree in the garden except one. Everything in creation has been gifted to Adam, with one exception—the tree of the knowledge of good and evil. God says, "But of the tree of the knowledge of good and evil you shall not eat, for in the day that you eat of it you shall surely die" (Gen 2:17 ESV).

Immediately after warning Adam about the reality of evil, God then speaks of something being "not good." After six "goods" and one "very good" in the first chapter, suddenly God says, "It is *not good* that the man should be alone" (2:18 ESV; emphasis added). From there we learn that the woman was made from the man's side and that he named her Eve (3:20). What do we make of these two instances, the assertion of evil and the "not good" of man being alone?

First, we recognize that God created the world to operate in a particular *way* but that there is an alternative. The way of evil was "possible" in the garden of God in Genesis 1 and 2, then was activated in the garden of God in Genesis 3. In Genesis 3, the crafty serpent speaks to the woman, asking, "Did God actually say, 'You shall not eat of any tree in the garden'?" (v. 1 ESV). Note that the serpent does not begin with flat contradiction of what God said. Rather, he begins by questioning. Only after the woman responds does the serpent directly contradict God's word by insisting, "You will not surely die. For God knows that when you eat of it your eyes will be opened, and you will be like God, knowing good and evil" (Gen 3:4–5 ESV). The other "way" is now clearly seen. There is another word, another story about what is right, good, and true in the world. The question is, Which story do you believe? Faith features strongly though subtly in Genesis 3 when the serpent puts an offer on the table. The serpent challenges God's word, the word that made the world, and the serpent dares the crown of God's creation, God's imagers, to believe another word, another story.

After hearing the serpent, the woman considers what she has heard. She sees that the fruit of the forbidden tree appears delicious and that desiring the tree will yield wisdom and insight, so she ate. Then she gives the fruit to her husband, and he eats it. Indeed, their eyes are opened. Immediately they realize they are naked. They have never experienced insecurity before. They have never felt a fear like this before. Suddenly they are seized with anxiety, worry, fretfulness, and hurry. They have disobeyed by believing and acting according to another word, a story other than God's. And immediately they seek to cover up. They sew fig leaves together and make loincloths to hide themselves. They have never felt the need to hide before, but things are different now.

How does God respond to this? This point in the story is filled with the anticipation of a child awaiting his father's punishment. The sound of footsteps coming down the hallway is terrifying for a child in trouble. Adam and Eve experience the same in the garden when they hear God walking. The Lord calls to the man, and Adam responds. He confesses that he was afraid because he was naked. God asks, "Who told you that you were naked? Did you eat from the tree that I commanded you not to eat from?" (Gen 3:11).

Notice that God's first question is "Who told you that you were naked?" He acknowledges another word, another story, another way, that opposes his word and way. The serpent's word was the word of a creature, not of the Creator. The serpent's word had no interest in "working and keeping" God's garden in accord with God's way. The serpent's word came with its own way, its own direction, its own view of the good, true, and beautiful. Much like "my way" that I insisted on as a toddler, the serpent's way may be desirable, but its end is death. Indeed, to follow "my way" is to follow the serpent's way.

The story picks up steam from this point forward as God curses the man, the woman, and the serpent and kicks Adam and Eve out of Eden forever. Things spiral downhill quickly after the first instance of human disobedience and sin in Genesis 3. Genesis 4 tells of the first murder, when Cain kills his brother Abel. The corruption increases, and by Genesis 6 God decides to destroy the earth and everything on it by flood with the exception of Noah, his family, and the animals on the ark.

After the flood, God covenants with Noah and the whole creation, promising that "never again will every creature be wiped out by floodwaters; there will never again be a flood to destroy the earth" (Gen 9:11). God then calls a man named Abram to be the father of a great nation that will bless the nations of the earth. God changed Abram's name to Abraham, promising him both a people and a place, a land where his people will dwell. God fulfilled this promise through Abraham's offspring including Isaac, Jacob, and Joseph. At the end of Genesis, Joseph is second in command of Egypt, the great superpower of that time, and things are looking up for God's people.

When the book of Exodus opens, many years have passed and the new king over Egypt does not remember Joseph. The Israelites, Abraham's descendants, are numerous and strong, and the king fears them. So, he makes them slaves. But God neither forgets his people nor his promise to Abraham. He raises up a man named Moses, an Israelite by birth who has been raised in Pharaoh's home, to confront Pharaoh and lead God's people out of slavery toward the land God had promised them. Eventually, God's people are released from Egypt, and as Pharaoh's army chases after them, God protects them by parting the waters of the Red Sea for his people to walk across on dry land, then crashes the waters down on Pharaoh's army, killing them all.

Though God performs great signs and wonders, his people are stubborn and slow to remember all that God has done. For forty years they wander in the desert due to their complaining and disobedience. Moses leads them until the time has come to enter the Promised Land, called Canaan. The book of Deuteronomy contains Moses's parting words to the people. He reminds them of their history and of the laws of God, and he warns them of what is to come, both good and bad.

Deuteronomy 10:12 is particularly insightful as Moses exhorts the people, "And now, Israel, what does the LORD your God ask of you except to fear the LORD your God *by walking in all his ways, to love him, and to worship the LORD your God with all your heart and all your soul?*" (italics added). Moses's words here are the equivalent of a pastor saying, "If you don't get anything else, get this!" Moses summarizes the very essence of what it means to follow God with these words. We may summarize further with *Fear him; love him; walk in his ways.*

Do you see the continuity with Genesis 1 and 2? Moses's command in Deut 10:12 is another way of saying, "Subdue and have dominion on the earth; work and keep the garden." We begin by believing what God has said about his world, then behaving in accordance with his Word and way in his world. To do otherwise is to believe another story, a false story, the serpent's story. To do otherwise is to cultivate another way in God's world, a way that opposes his way. Moses said to fear God (for this is the beginning of knowledge and wisdom), love him (for this is the greatest commandment), and walk in his ways (for this is our God-given responsibility of exercising dominion in his world). And this has not changed. Though the world is complicated by sin, God's imagers are still called to promote and preserve God's way in the world.

As the story continues, God's people are established in the land of Canaan, but they regularly forget the Lord their God. They pursue foreign gods and foreign women, they fail to obey God's law, and they insist that God give them a king like the other nations. God obliges and establishes a monarchy in Israel. On the whole, the monarchy is one disaster after another until the kingdom is divided in two, and eventually both the north and south are overtaken and exiled. God uses the monarchy, however, to fulfill his plan of raising up David, for example, a man after God's own heart. Though David is far from perfect, God covenants with him, promising a future King who will sit on David's throne forever. David's son Solomon appears to be this promised king at first, but he is drawn away by his desire for women and the monarchy continues in decline. It appears God has forgotten his people and his promise. But God brings beauty from ashes. Even back in Genesis 3 when God cursed the man, woman, and serpent, he placed a promise amid the punishment. He promised that from Eve would come One who would crush the head of the serpent (Gen 3:15). He is the One promised to bless the nations through Abraham; the One greater than Moses who will lead God's people out of an even greater slavery; a King mightier than David who will not fall to temptation; One wiser than Solomon who will be called the Mighty God, everlasting Father, Prince of Peace. He is the One who will confront the word of the serpent and reestablish the way of the Lord.

Interlude on Culture

First, do not overlook God's use of cultural means to fulfill his plan and accomplish his purposes. To begin, God's promises were culturally communicated and culturally fulfilled. For example, his use of language (not to mention Egyptian social structures, sacrificial practices, and navigation by boat) to communicate his messages of promise to Noah, Abraham, and Moses confirms that God's promises were communicated and fulfilled in particular cultural contexts. God did not deploy a plan of salvation outside creation. Rather, he engaged specific times and places in his creation, even inhabiting his creation in the person of Jesus, to redeem and restore the way of creation.

Second, Israel's task was cultural. Through the prophets, God passionately called his people to "return to me, and I will return to you" (Mal 3:7b). The failure of God's people may be generally described as a failure to walk in his ways. Specifically, their sins were cultural expressions of insincere worship, sacrificing to false gods, rampant divorce, failure of priests and leaders to uphold the Law, and even robbing God by failing to contribute tithes and offerings. The Lord promised punishment and the terrible (yet glorious!) day of the Lord to come, complete with the King who will rule over all the earth (Zech 14:9). All of this—the good and the bad—is cultural.

The overarching failure of God's people was the advancing of a false way, a cultural expression of death and opposition to God. Yet God's restoration was also cultural—an eternal kingdom where war weapons become farm tools, sadness ceases, and every nation on earth worships Christ the King. Even when exiled by the Babylonians—a neighboring evil culture— Jeremiah instructed God's people to exhibit the way of God and

> build houses and live in them. Plant gardens and eat their produce. Find wives for yourselves, and have sons and daughters. Find wives for your sons and give your daughters to men in marriage so that they bear sons and daughters . . . Pursue the well-being of the city I have deported you to. Pray to the LORD on its behalf, for when it thrives, you will thrive. (Jer 29:5–7)

Christ the Way

The pages of the New Testament open with Matthew reciting the genealogy of Jesus of Nazareth to demonstrate his family connection to the line of Abraham and David. This is followed by the story of his birth to the virgin Mary, who was betrothed to Joseph but not yet married. Matthew made clear that Jesus's virgin birth was to fulfill the promise of the prophet Isaiah: "'Behold, the virgin shall conceive and bear a son, and they shall call his name Immanuel' (which means, God with us)" (Matt 1:23 ESV).

Clearly, this was not just any ordinary child. This child was of the lineage of David, born of a virgin as foretold, celebrated by the angels, and visited by wise men from the east. Moreover, at an early age this child confounded the teachers at the temple in Jerusalem with his understanding of the Scriptures. Then his first cousin, whom we know as John the Baptist, dedicated his life to declaring that the Christ was coming. John was sent as Isaiah and Zechariah had prophesied as "the voice of one crying in the wilderness: 'Prepare the way of the Lord, make his paths straight'" (Luke 3:4 ESV).

"The way of the Lord." An interesting phrase spoken by the prophet Isaiah about the future ministry of John the Baptist. John was preparing the *way* of the Lord. But what is this way? In short, the *way* is not first a "what." It is a "who." As Jesus declared about himself in John 14:6, "I am the way, and the truth, and the life. No one comes to the Father except through me" (ESV). In his excellent book *The Jesus Way*, Eugene Peterson writes, "Jesus is an alternative to the dominant ways of the world, not a supplement to them. We cannot use impersonal means to do or say a personal thing—and the gospel is personal or it is nothing."[8] We must not miss this point. Jesus is the way of God in the flesh. And this is the *way* in which we are called to walk. Peterson elaborates further:

> So. Jesus the Way, the ways of Jesus. He shows the way. He also *is* the way. He doesn't point out the way and then step aside and let us get there on our own as best we can. Jesus points out the way, but then he takes the initiative, inviting us to go with him, taking us with him across land and sea, through all kinds of weather, avoiding dead ends and seductive byways, watching out for danger and alerting us to enemies.[9]

Briefly then, we highlight three essential connections between Jesus and the way regarding the biblical story and our place in it. First, *Jesus restored the way of the Lord through his life and work.* As John the Baptist prepared the way of the Lord, Jesus reestablished the way of the Lord in the world *in himself.* As Peterson asserts in the preceding quote, the way of the Lord was not some five-step method for a happy and fulfilling life that Jesus pointed us toward. Nor was it merely an inspiring life and death that he compelled religious zealots to pursue. Restoring and reestablishing the way of the Lord was and is *personal.* Jesus's virgin birth reset the dial of humanity's sin affliction. His perfect life made possible his acceptance as a spotless sacrifice to God. His death was a headfirst assault on

---

[8] Eugene Peterson, *The Jesus Way: A Conversation on the Ways That Jesus Is the Way* (Grand Rapids: Eerdmans, 2011), ii.

[9] Peterson, 36.

the great enemy of all creation because Jesus handed himself over to the enemy and became sin for us (2 Cor 5:21). His resurrection dealt the death blow to death itself. Jesus turned our greatest enemy, death, into good news. He brought life out of death, restoring the way of our humanity and the way of God in the world.

Second, the good news of Jesus restores the way of the Lord in us, his imagers. The impact of Jesus's life and work did not end with reestablishing the way of the Lord in the creation broadly. It restored the way for all of humanity—male and female—to fulfill our original purpose as imagers of God to multiply and fill the earth, to subdue the earth and have dominion over it. Dominion, not domination. Our job in God's world is to steward all things seen and unseen before the Creator, advancing his ways in his world. This was impossible as long as we were enslaved to sin. But now "the law of the Spirit of life has set [us] free in Christ Jesus from the law of sin and death" (Rom 8:2 ESV). So now we live not *according to* the flesh but *according to the Spirit* while remaining in the flesh. The language here is precise and intentional. This is not a dualistic approach to life that suggests spirit *over* flesh. It is a spirit-first approach that understands God's grace as restoring our nature in Christ by the power of the Spirit. Now we offer our bodies (that is, our lives) as living sacrifices in all of life (Rom 12:1–2).

Third, the way of the Lord is our ancient-new purpose in the world. Our way in the world is not a new way. It is an old way, the original way of God, renewed for today. This old-new way is similar to Jesus's words in John 13:34–35: "I give you a new command: Love one another. Just as I have loved you, you are also to love one another. By this everyone will know that you are my disciples, if you love one another." This commandment is not new in that God's people have never been commanded to love one another before. Rather, it's new in the sense that it is an old command made new for today. Jesus's life and work inaugurated the process of all things being made new. The way of God that was established in the beginning—and challenged and misdirected by sin—has been reestablished and made new in Jesus. Now we walk worthy of our calling in Christ. We walk in the way of God.

A Kingdom Interlude

Jesus's announcement of the kingdom happened in real time and space, a real culture with all the bells and smells associated with first-century, Middle Eastern, Jewish culture. Jesus's hometown was small and not well respected (as suggested by Nathaniel's question in John 1:46, "Can anything good come out of Nazareth?"). This underscores the cultural associations of Jesus's time and place. It was not a bustling economic center, the home of intellectual elites, nor did it boast an influential arts community. It was a small town with one water supply near the border of Samaria in lower Galilee. Not where one might expect a world-changer to hail from. Yet Nazareth, meaning "branch," was the hometown of Jesus, the "root" of Jesse.

In Jesus's day, as in our own, government authorities loomed large. Earthly kingdoms call for ultimate allegiance and expect citizens to embody the way of that kingdom. Jesus's time and place was a web of Jewish and Roman cultures that at times cooperated and at other times competed against one another. Thus, when Jesus began preaching about the kingdom, he seized the attention of the Jews who were awaiting the reestablishment of the kingdom, and he gained the attention of the Romans, who had everything to lose if in fact a new kingdom were established.

In his Sermon on the Mount, his longest single teaching in the New Testament, Jesus issued a new way of life—the way of life in God's kingdom. He began by describing the blessed life— an echo to the psalms, especially the righteous one of Psalm 1— but this blessed life was not what the hearers expected. Rather than a vision of the biggest, fastest, strongest, richest, and most powerful, Jesus offered a vision of the small, slow, weak, poor, and persecuted. These, Jesus insisted, will inherit the kingdom of heaven. And the pure in heart will "see God" (Matt 5:8).

This kingdom way of life followed the way of Jesus, taking the low place rather than seeking the place of prominence, and attended to prominent areas of both personal and public sin such as anger, lust, and divorce. Jesus teaches us how to pray, centered on the call for God's kingdom and will to come on earth as they are in heaven. He challenges us to love our enemies and not to worry or be anxious but to know the peace-filled provision of God by faith. He ended his sermon with a familiar two-way metaphor—our houses (our lives) are built either on sand or on rock. The sandy foundation is chosen by those who refuse to hear and obey Jesus's teaching. The rock is the chosen foundation of those who believe and obey.

This way of life was not the norm for Jesus's day. Jesus's culture was full of self-centered, power hungry, anxious, and insecure religious do-gooders—quite similar to our own. The way of the kingdom, however, is the way of submission and dependence on God, of denying oneself, of considering the interests of others above our own. The way of the kingdom is the way of the cross.

The Way Eternal

Christians are to pursue the "more excellent way" of love as Paul wrote in 1 Corinthians 12–13. He ended that chapter reminding us that "faith, hope, and love abide, these three; but the greatest of these is love" (1 Cor 13:13 ESV). Faith anchors us in the time and space reality of Jesus, who came to earth, lived perfectly, died unjustly on our behalf, then defeated death and hell in his resurrection. This story is true in every sense of the word. And our faith is anchored in that reality. Hope serves like a beacon for the future return of Christ. Similar to Paul's argument in 1 Thess 4:13–15, as much confidence as we have in Jesus's resurrection (a past event), this much confidence we also have in his coming again (a future event). And this is our hope. If we doubt Jesus's return, then we must doubt his resurrection, and vice-versa. Indeed, if he rose from the dead and ascended to the Father, we can be certain that his return is sure. While our faith is anchored in promise of our past, our hope is fixed in the promise of our future.

What of love, then? One might suggest, as Saint Augustine did, that love is greatest because it is the only one of the three that is eternal. For in the new heaven and new earth, we will no longer need faith and hope, but love will always remain.[10] We think Augustine is on to something here. The way of God

---

[10] Augustine, *Teaching Christianity (De Doctrina Christiana)*, vol. 1, trans. Edmund Hill (New York: New City, 1995), 38, 42.

was built into God's purpose and direction for creation from the beginning. Though this purpose and direction were compromised by sin, God in his wisdom and grace sent Jesus, the way and wisdom of God, to restore the way of the Lord in the world *in himself!* This way is nothing if not the way of love. After all, Jesus insisted that the greatest commandment is love for God and neighbor.

We should not expect this commandment to love to cease in eternity. Rather, while specifics about the new heaven and earth remain largely a mystery, we should expect that eternity will be filled with real people and will be a real material place, a time known as "forever" where we experience a new creation unstained by sin and characterized by the way of God, the way of love, for eternity. In our current corruptible form, such a world is impossible to imagine. But we can be sure that the new heaven and earth will be awash at all times and in all places with culture, the culture that is the way of Christ, the way of love.

Conclusion: Now What?

Why all the attention to the biblical story when we live in the here and now? Because it is, in fact, the *true story of the whole world*. It isn't merely the story of God; it is the story of us *here and now*. Christian, this is your story. A story of where you are from, where you are going, and the reality about how you are to live and love until Christ returns. Just as Jesus taught us to pray, "Thy Kingdom come, Thy will be done in earth, as it is in heaven" (Matt 6:10 KJV), we seek to advance the ways of the King in all of creation, in all of culture, in the whole of the kingdom.

2

Culture Defined

Culture is religion made visible; it is religion
actualized in the innumerable relations of daily life.
—J. H. Bavinck, *The Impact of Christianity*
on the Non-Christian World

As we outlined in the previous chapter, from the beginning of creation, God's people have been called to advance the ways the King and his kingdom. This calling has all of life in scope, for the Genesis 1 and 2 command has the whole of God's creation in view when God commands Adam and Eve to fill the earth with his imagers and have dominion over it.

This command is cultural through and through. Obedience to this command always results in culture—but disobedience to this divine command also always results in culture.

What is culture, anyway, and why does God's mandate for human life in his creation have culture in view? In this chapter we will explore ways culture is defined, then offer a definition that will guide our discussion for the rest of the book. We have argued that God's work throughout history begins with a creation made for his glory and culminates in a restoration of this creation when it is set free from the misdirection of sin. This narrative of Scripture offers a vision that helps Christians make sense of all the particulars of our lives. It offers a way to follow Christ in his ways and wisdom for life.

What Is Culture?

The lexical roots of the word *culture* fall very close to this imagery of God's very first instructions to humanity to work the ground. The Latin origin of the English word is *cultura*, which comes from the verb *colere*, meaning to "inhabit, cultivate, protect, honour with worship."[1] The range of meaning associated with these words is decidedly agrarian and has to do with tending to something, from which we inherit our English verb "to cultivate."

When we think about what we usually call "culture," this makes good sense. In everyday usage, we say that language or customs are part of someone's culture, and these are things that are crafted over time by societies. Culture can also refer to a whole category of our lives, such as the arts. Someone is said to be engaged in the creation of high culture when they author a significant play or film, compose a stirring piece of music, or write a novel. All of these are works of creative imagination, forming something meaningful and truly beautiful from

---

[1] Raymond Williams, *Keywords: A Vocabulary of Culture and Society*, rev. ed. (New York: Oxford University, 1976), 77.

the seemingly raw materials of words, sounds, rhythms, colors, and textures.

But in a technical sense, culture is more than merely these specific works that are especially impactful for taste or beauty or how we identify ourselves in relation to others. When missionaries prepare to transition to a new place for ministry, they must learn about the cultural context in which they plan to serve. Additionally, we often refer to the whole swathe of society around us as "the culture," as if it is something to resist or to celebrate or to reform. All of these uses of the word point to an important observation: culture is something that is all around us and in which we are immersed. It is as inescapable as breathing, a universal part of human life. In fact, we might say that culture is the language of life we speak to understand and give meaning to life. Everything we do is cultural, and everything we think and say is conveyed through culture.

Definition of *Culture*

So here is our definition of culture: *culture consists of the ways and products of creatures in creation.* Let us unpack this piece by piece, going in reverse order. First, as the ways and products of "creatures," culture is something all creatures do as part of their mode of living—and not just human creatures. Certainly not all creaturely actions are cultural, but there are examples from nature in which animals cultivate things on purpose to achieve a particular goal. Woodcutter ants create an amazing type of culture. They bite off pieces of leaves and carry them back to their nests to feed colonies of fungus, which in turn provide them with food throughout the year. African elephants create something like culture when the matriarchs in the herd pass down through generations memories of all the hidden watering holes across the arid desert. Likewise, certain chimpanzee colonies have been found to use tools made from sticks that they teach other members of the colony to use, which are unique to that colony.

As amazing as these ways and products of nonhuman creatures are, however, the culture of human creatures is on another level altogether. Only human beings uniquely create culture as a function of their identity as imagers of God because we are tasked with ordering his creation according to his ways. Only humans can know God personally—that is, knowing him as a being who personally reveals himself to us to be known—and therefore only humans can create rich patterns of meaning to organize life in ways that reflect who he is.

Second, implied in the idea of "products" is the idea of production. The creation of culture involves the *doing* of something by creatures capable of *doing things*, that is, producing things. Certainly, flowers and bees both produce things. Flowers produce pollen and nectar, and bees use both to produce honey. So, does that mean everything that grows and reproduces in the natural world is culture? We think not. Rather, the way the word "culture" is usually used, which is how we are using it here, sees the "cultivation" of something as requiring a *cultivator*. That is, a creature capable of thought, deciding to do something on purpose. Interacting with God's creation, perceiving the world around us and reacting, even if only cognitively in our minds, is necessary for culture to emerge. Culture does not arise spontaneously in the field or forest, like a dandelion or pine tree might. Culture is natural in the sense that it is made of the "stuff" of creation, but only through there being something or someone who shapes and creates it. Culture results from an act of the will, a creature choosing to do this or do that. As they say, Mozart's symphonies do not grow on trees.

The same can be said about the idea of "ways." To walk a certain way or path, or to walk in a certain manner or style, requires a creature to be capable of going this way or that, to skip or cartwheel or bear crawl. But "ways" also communicates a further layer of meaning we think is important in defining culture. Ways communicates a type of order to doing things in a certain manner. It implies purposefulness and meaning. Ants do not feed fungus for no reason; they do it so they can eat. Elephants do not show their young where to dig in the dirt for nothing, but so that they can teach them where to find underground springs. Likewise, human beings plant seeds in furrows of earth so that water might drain where the roots might benefit most from it. Cultural acts are things done on purpose, with meaning and intent.

As fascinating as it would be to study nonhuman culture, though, let us limit our focus to human culture. Even in the range of all the things humans do in creation, are all actions by humans cultural? In a certain sense, we would answer no. Some actions are instinctual responses that we do not do on purpose but rather as a gut reaction to something that happens around us. On a hot day we guzzle water to quench our thirst. What could be more natural than that? However, nothing we do or think is ever devoid of cultural influences. What we drink, in what way, from what vessel, and even our reflections on why we do drink and how we ought to do it again are all cast in cultural forms that either we create ourselves or are given to us by the

ways other people do these actions. As reflecting creatures trying to make sense of the world around us, we are cultural beings
through and through.

Put another way, we might say that cultural patterns of
thought and action are worlds of meaning that are not only
formed by us but also form us and teach us how to make our
way in the world.[2] The stuff of culture, the language we speak in
these worlds of meaning, consists of forms and artifacts. Forms
are the patterns of thought, the habits we enact, or the values
we assign to different things in life. Songs we sing to our children, routines that organize our early morning commutes, or the
motivations driving how we study for a test are all cultural forms.

Artifacts are what we make; they are culture made tangible
in the ways we apply ourselves to the creation of them. Cell
phones, paper airplanes, compost piles, and cheese boards are
all artifacts of culture that exist even after we have finished creating them. All of these things are what result when we interact
meaningfully with God's creation, in the way that he has made
us to live in his image. Additionally, acknowledging culture as
the forms or artifacts of human beings means that culture is an
extension of ourselves upon creation. As such, just as we can
choose to walk in Christ's way or to walk the way of folly, so
culture always advances the ways of Christ or not.

Finally, we have said this already, but it stands to be rein-
forced: cultural meaning moves in two ways. Not only do we

---

[2] Kevin J. Vanhoozer, "What Is Everyday Theology? How and Why
Christians Should Read Culture," in *Everyday Theology: How to Read
Cultural Texts and Interpret Trends*, ed. Kevin J. Vanhoozer, Charles A.
Anderson, and Michael J. Sleasman (Grand Rapids: Baker Academic,
2007), 26.

create culture and thus communicate meaning upon or through the created order, so also are we always receiving it from others. We are constantly shaped by the cultural forms and artifacts all around us, and these in turn inform our own culture making. Culture is never a solitary endeavor.

Approaches to Culture

We have been describing what culture is, but how should we think about culture? What use is this for helping us understand how to follow the ways of Christ in the story he is telling throughout history? More important, what should our posture be toward cultural life in the various contexts we find ourselves? For those who study culture formally, there are different approaches to describing what culture is and what value it has for reflecting on human life. Each of these may offer us helpful insights into how to think Christianly about culture in order to know how best to live after Christ. You might encounter these approaches in different types of disciplined reflection on what culture is, but each approach alone does not provide the full picture. So we would like to offer another way.

Sociological: The Social Scientist

A sociological approach to culture is what might appear in anthropological studies of various tribes or people groups around the world. This approach takes culture as simply a natural fact of life. As such, culture is something to be studied. This approach sees the cultural forms and artifacts a group of people embrace as something to be used to predict the motivations, values, and actions of individuals in a given context.[3] Studying how a tribe of people talk about their ancestors may offer insight into how those people think about their identity in relation to others and how they treat outsiders. Culture in this sense is used to account for why we do certain things in a particular way.

Missiological: The Missionary

A missiological approach sees culture as a pathway for action instead of merely describing patterns of human behavior. Missionaries see culture as a strategy for how to best adapt the message of the Bible to ways that will most make sense to a target group of people.[4] Culture in this sense is something to be used to create something new, like an evangelism strategy or new liturgies for worship in a church.

Ethical: The Culture Warrior

A third approach takes an ethical stance toward analyzing whether cultural forms are good or bad. For this approach, culture is something that is "out there," beyond us, and is a product of worldviews and convictions that Christians must understand in order to either resist its influence or collaborate

---

[3] Roy D'Andrade offers a survey of various sociological models of culture and their use in the study of various people groups. Roy D'Andrade, "Some Kinds of Causal Power That Make up Culture," in *Explaining Culture Scientifically*, ed. Melissa J. Brown (Seattle: University of Washington, 2008), 19–36.

[4] For a helpful summary of various approaches within this model, see A. Scott Moreau, *Contextualization in World Missions: Mapping and Assessing Evangelical Models* (Grand Rapids: Kregel, 2012).

with it.[5] Culture is embodied in music, voting ballot issues, spending habits, sports, and so forth. The task of the Christian is to judge what precommitments and meanings are communicated through these and if they align with what God has said in Scripture. Thus, in this approach, culture is something to be judged in order to inform us how to respond to it.

A Fourth Way: The Blended Approach

In an effort to draw upon the strengths of each of these, we offer in this book a blended approach. If we begin with the conviction that Scripture shows that human beings are made to image God through culture, then culture is simply a way of life for creatures who exist in God's creation. We might call this a creational or phenomenological approach to culture. This approach recognizes that culture itself is a fact of creaturely existence, and as such it is included with what God celebrates when he pronounces his creation very good (Gen 1:31–2:3). But like a tool in the hand of either a robber or a plumber, it can be directed in ways that go against God's pattern for life.

---

[5] We hesitate to offer an example of this approach, as often this mindset is well-intentioned but fails to explore the way their own approach to a "Christian worldview" is itself culturally embedded. A hallmark of this approach, then, is the mindset that "the culture" is society at large and is fundamentally anti-Christian and that the Christian task of cultural engagement is to confront "the culture" with the true claims of Christian faith. Our hope in presenting our model is to validate some of this approach while at the same time deepening our understanding of what culture is and how it relates to the Christian life.

We might say that, like language or tools, culture as a thing is morally ambiguous. Taken in isolation, because culture can be used for good or evil, imbued with right or wrong meaning, its moral status is not determined until we look at specific examples of culture. Just as there are two paths in life, the way of Christ and wisdom or the way of evil and folly, so culture is subject to the choices we make. Culture is given by God as the way in which we either image him in obedience or obscure his image through sin. This means that culture itself can never be an ultimate good, nor can it be held as the final goal of the Christian life. Culture is what is involved with being on the way with Christ; it is not the destination. Certainly, the goal of creation is not devoid of culture. The story of Scripture opens with a garden, something cultivated by God and given to humanity to keep charge over. It ends in Revelation in a city, constructed in a new creation, filled with buildings, feasts, languages, and song.

However, culture itself is not the point. Knowing God as he has revealed himself and being united to him together with his people for his glory is the goal. Culture is ever-present on the way to life eternal in his city. It is the language of the story he is telling through his people, in his incarnation in Christ, and by his church as they make disciples of all nations. Many may seek to argue that the cultural mandate is about the creation of culture. But the mandate of Genesis 1 is to glorify God and multiply his image throughout the creation. Culture reveals; it either makes manifest before us the ways of God or the ways of folly, and often it is a mixture of both. As such, culture is not the *telos* for human life before God. It is the necessary means to the good end of God's people living by God's ways in his presence.

This is not the posture toward culture that Christians have always embodied. In the next chapter we will consider different attitudes toward culture and the cultural task that Christians have exhibited. For now, we stress that—while culture is something that tells us much about how people understand the world around them and their place in it, and that we often must make value judgments about what is good or bad in given cultures and strategize about how to engage with these—we must begin by understanding culture's proper place in God's story with creation.

Patterns of Meaning on the Way

Returning to the observation that culture consists of worlds of meaning that help us inhabit God's creation, either in line with the purposes for which he made us or against them, let us consider different types of culture. This will establish the scope of what we are describing as cultural and therefore worthy of careful reflection on how to follow Christ in all of life. A clear understanding of culture enables us to make sense of our place in the world and helps us to discern meaning in life. Through culture we receive the most basic elements of our beliefs about the world: Where did all of this come from, where is it going, who are we, and how are we to live in light of this? In turn, we reenact these foundational beliefs about the world through our own creation of culture, through the things we make, the way we speak, the motivations behind our actions, and how we understand ourselves in relation to others.

High Culture

As we mentioned, many people associate the word *culture* with elements of high culture, which consists of the arts, such as theater, literature, cinema, classical music, or visual art. Not only are these elements windows into the creative imagination of a people that show us what they find beautiful or worthy of celebration, but also they are works that influence us into seeing the world in a certain way. For example, the famous Jewish scholar of language and literature, Erich Auerbach, argues that the way authors of classic works of literature in the Western tradition present the world tells us much about how the Judeo-Christian view of God and the meaning of life imparted by his hand of providence has defined Western culture's understanding of individual natural rights and democratic agency that has come to characterize our culture.[6] The way figures like Dante or Shakespeare represent reality in their writings shapes the values mimicked by our culture as those works leave their mark on our values and ways of thinking.

Pop Culture

While high culture has historically had an outsized influence on the social imagination of Western society, arguably now this role has been taken over by pop culture. Notoriously difficult to define, pop culture might simply be called "the everyday culture of everyday people."[7] It consists of trends and tastes

---

[6] Erich Auerbach, *Mimesis: The Representation of Reality in Western Literature* (Princeton, NJ: Princeton University, 2003).

[7] Vanhoozer, "What Is Everyday Theology?," 27.

magnified by media channels that predominate in our society, such as top forty music charts or the latest films or trending shows streaming on Netflix. It also consists of what the social media influencers are telling us to consume by their words, the actions we are invited to mimic, or what they are themselves consuming. If culture forms us in worlds of meaning, pop culture represents a window into the aesthetic tastes, moral sentiments, and even political causes that pop cultural creators embrace and seek to monetize for the masses. We are taught to value romantic love, self-authenticity, and purchasing car insurance "in fifteen minutes or less" by the narratives about life crafted for us by savvy marketers—and usually the under-lying pretext is that we will not be truly happy unless we buy their products and services.

So powerful are the worlds of meaning constructed by pop culture that a group of twentieth-century Marxists thought that pop culture was a potent tool of controlling the masses that was preventing the attainment of true justice by inhibiting the societal revolution that never came. Known as the Frankfurt School, this approach is represented in the works of scholars like Theodor Adorno and Herbert Marcuse.[8] They believed that by taking hold of the popular culture-forming institutions of society, they could reshape society for activism that would peacefully lead to utopia. Seeing the way corporations and media makers have so embraced radical ideas on sexuality,

---

[8] For a helpful introduction to the Frankfurt School and how it has influenced our contemporary culture in the West, see Carl R. Trueman, *The Rise and Triumph of the Modern Self: Cultural Amnesia, Expressive Individualism, and the Road to Sexual Revolution* (Wheaton, IL: Crossway, 2020).

especially during June for Pride Month, makes one wonder
if their strategies have succeeded in reshaping the world in
which we live.

Ordinary Culture

However much we associate the idea of culture with pop culture, all of life is cultural. This means that the most widespread
example of culture is actually the mundane cultures we create
and inhabit in the myriad of ordinary activities that characterize
our lives. Many people are not used to thinking of their everyday
habits and routines in cultural terms, but those habits and routines reveal much about how we think we ought to inhabit the
world around us. Mowing the yard, washing the dishes, doing
homework, walking the dog, putting children to bed, sleeping in,
reading a book, and watching the sunset are all culture-forming
acts. In some degree they reveal our motivations, desires, priorities, and fears. Not only this, by engaging in them in ways that
are patterned on what other people do, we shape our lives in
line with the worlds of meaning we receive from others. Culture
is something we receive as well as something we give, and all of
it together orders life in untold ways.

Impactful Culture

Still, there is a sense that some cultural labors are more impactful than others on large groups of people. That is, some products of cultural labor are more directly responsible for shaping
the worlds of meaning conveyed by culture. This does not mean
that in the eyes of God such cultural forms are more valuable,

but it does help explain why the impact of certain actions is felt more broadly and for longer than others.

Changing a diaper, though seemingly mundane, is a magnificent act of culture. Even if they do not realize it, parents honor God and profess his ways when they care for the needs of their little ones, even if it takes twenty-five wipes to do it! But compare this to Plato's *Republic*, which for millennia has shaped the way people think about knowledge, the world, and our place in it. When considering the phenomenon of certain cultural creations, it is clear that some cultural creations have a more profound impact on society at large. Some expressions of culture are more directly responsible for shaping the patterns of meaning each of us receive and use to inhabit our own cultural contexts. This certainly does not mean that these expressions of culture are somehow better or inherently more important. Rather, like the Gettysburg Address compared to your last Twitter post, it means that some expressions of culture are more enduring and have a broader impact than others.

Conclusion: The Significance of Culture for the Christian Life

In this chapter we have argued that all of life is cultural and that this is the result of God's good design for human life. The mode of existence for human beings, made in his image, is cultural. For culture is what results when human beings order the world around them into something meaningful. Not only is this true of the pop culture of Instagram influencers or the high culture of painters and sculptors, but it is also true of the daycare worker, accountant, parent, and farmer. If the story God is telling through Scripture and history concerns the way of Christ, then the manner in which we walk is always through cultural forms.

This means that every form of cultural labor, no matter how mundane, is important for our consideration as we seek to follow Christ in his ways. Throughout the rest of this book, we will explore the theological foundations of this conclusion more deeply and then offer a framework for how to walk Christ's way, in any time and place, that we might glorify him and be formed more clearly—and *culturally*—in his image.

3

Typologies of Culture

Everything is from God, who has reconciled
us to himself through Christ and has given
us the ministry of reconciliation.
                                —2 Corinthians 5:18

In the previous chapter we defined culture, evaluated four
approaches to culture, and argued that all of life is cultural
and wrought with meaning. Christians throughout history have
exemplified different stances toward their cultural context.
Scholars writing on theology and culture have provided typologies of how Christians have related to culture. In this chapter
we consider some of the most influential of these typologies and
weigh their strengths and weaknesses.

Each set of typologies attempts to account for the differences in cultural attitude exhibited by Christians in various contexts, and these typologies do so by highlighting how Christians

tell the story of God and his creation and by deducing cultural habits and priorities from there. This is fundamentally the right approach. How we tell the story of God's work in history and then how we find ourselves in it is the starting point for Christian cultural engagement because that is where the Bible both starts and ends the story. But, as they say, the devil is in the details. *How* we put together the pieces of the story, which elements we foreground and why, will result in very different cultural trajectories for our lives in the world. After we look at how various Christians in history have put together the pieces of the story, we will offer in the subsequent chapters our own framework as a way forward.

Typologies of Culture

Through the centuries, Christians have related to their surrounding societies and cultures in a variety of ways. In the early centuries of the church, many Christians throughout the Roman Empire held that they possessed clear responsibilities to the poor and sick, and they even rescued infants abandoned by their pagan parents.[1] They had businesses, learned trades, and worked alongside their non-Christian neighbors, often seeking to be model citizens of society. But for many, there were clear boundaries separating what type of cultural participation was permissible and what was impermissible for Christians. In Corinth, Christians in Paul's day debated whether it was appropriate to eat meat that had been used in pagan rituals

---

[1] See Tertullian, *Apology*, 39. *ANF* 3:47; Augustine, "Letter XCVIII," *NPNF1*, 1:406–10.

(1 Cor 8:1–13). Later, Christians held military service to be off-limits because of the requirement to participate in the worship of the emperor.

All of this shows the early church's overall posture toward the cultural life of the church's surrounding context and reveals that, since the first century, Christians have wrestled with what their attitude toward culture ought to be. In the centuries that followed, many Christians in the Roman and Byzantine empires and beyond developed entirely different postures. Some fled to the desert to devote themselves to the contemplative life and escape the decadence of those cultures. Over a millennium later, some European Christians in the Anabaptist movement would also separate themselves, building their own communities set apart from society. Still others, such as those who embraced the social gospel movement at the turn of the twentieth century, understood the Christian faith to be fundamentally concerned with societal justice and service to the poor. They saw this as requiring Christians to be activists within every cultural context to root out its inequities. Taking this a step further, the Latin American Christians who developed Liberation Theology held that Christianity's posture toward culture is to be revolutionary, using political means and even armed resistance if necessary to change culture.

These examples all reveal that Christians throughout the ages have embraced many different attitudes toward culture, from politics to economic realities, education and the arts, and even leisure activities such as sports. In the past century, theologians and social thinkers have offered different models to describe these different cultural attitudes and have sought to make sense of them by proposing various motivations that gave rise to those attitudes. We can call these differences "typologies" of Christianity and culture. As several of these have been influential in shaping how we talk about faith and culture today, it is helpful to see how these typologies focus on different elements of the biblical narrative as the central framework for explaining why Christians often think so differently about culture.

Ernst Troeltsch and the Church and Culture Typology

One of the first people to offer a typology of how Christians relate to culture was the German theologian Ernst Troeltsch in the early twentieth century.[2] Troeltsch argued that what determines how Christians inhabit society is how they think about the nature of the church. This led Troeltsch to posit three models of what the church is.

The Church Type

The first, formally named the "church type," conceives of the church as an institution that is given the means of salvation, and its task is to mediate that salvation to the world. An example of this would be the Roman Catholic Church. This type understands church membership to include salvific participation

---

[2] Ernst Troeltsch, *The Social Teaching of the Christian Churches*, trans. Olive Wyon, 2 vols. (New York: MacMillan, 1931). Long provides a helpful summary of Troeltsch's typology. See D. Stephen Long, *Theology and Culture: A Guide to the Discussion* (Eugene, OR: Cascade, 2008), 56–58.

in the sacraments (such as baptism and the Lord's Supper). According to Troeltsch, in this model the church's role in culture is to be a culture-forming institution with authority over society like the state's, to save society with its sacraments.

The Sect Type

The second type Troeltsch names is the "sect type," which understands the church as a voluntary gathering of individuals made up of true believers who profess faith in Christ. Accordingly, the church's purpose in the world is to call others to be saved. This leads to a stance toward culture that leads Christians to retreat into the walls of the church in order to focus on the inner spiritual life, which concerns the faith the church confesses. An example of this type would be Anabaptists, or even Congregationalists, whom Troeltsch saw as oriented only toward a fundamentalist isolation from culture.

The Mystic Type

The third type is the "mystic type," which focuses on the inner experience of faith that is not defined by any objective doctrine or confession but rather by the feeling of being connected to the divine. In this model, the church neither believes it possesses authority over culture nor retreats from culture, but rather, it draws upon culture for its inspiration as it dwells amid culture. As a classic German Liberal, Troeltsch favored this approach because it accurately describes the characteristics of the mainline Protestant tradition to which he belonged.

TROELTSCH'S CHURCH AND CULTURE TYPOLOGY

Type	Description	Example
The Church Type	The Church brings salvation and therefore has authority over the culture.	Roman Catholic Church
The Sect Type	The Church voluntarily gathers itself out of the culture.	Anabaptists
The Mystic Type	The Church "feels" God in and through the culture.	Classic Theological Liberals

Assessment

Troeltsch's typology is helpful for two reasons. First, Troeltsch helped inspire later thinkers by providing models of cultural attitudes and tracing how these models result in various motivations and stances toward culture, which Christians embrace as they approach life in society. Troeltsch therefore turns our attention to the question of how Christians should live in the world by helping to account for the reasons why Christians often have such different views on culture. Second, Troeltsch points to differences in core beliefs of Christians about the biblical narrative, specifically how to think about what the church is and how it fits in God's story. In providing our own models of how Christians relate to culture, we will follow Troeltsch's example. However, Troeltsch ultimately gets it wrong when he argues that the only way for Christians to have the proper relationship to culture is to understand the Christian faith as based on a subjective feeling of

God, rather than on the knowledge of what God has done in history and revealed about himself through his historically spoken word in Scripture.

Richard Niebuhr and the Christ and Culture Typology

Perhaps the most influential typology today comes from Richard Niebuhr. Whereas Troeltsch examines the question of Christians and culture through the lens of the nature of the church, Niebuhr provides a typology focused on Christ. For Niebuhr, the way Christians have answered the question of how they are to relate to civilization proceeds from how they understand how the incarnate Christ of Scripture related to culture.[3] Because the Bible provides a complex picture of Christ's cultural existence, however, Christians have disagreed over which parts of the Bible provide the interpretive key by which to read all of the others. Accordingly, Niebuhr examines five different models and associates historical figures with them for articulating Christ's relationship to culture from the text.

Christ against Culture

The first is the "Christ against Culture" type, which sees Christ's warning to resist the world, coupled with John's call not to love the world (1 John 2:15), as setting the terms for life in culture. Though Niebuhr does not give this type a formal

---

[3] Richard Niebuhr, *Christ and Culture*, 50th anniversary expanded ed. (San Francisco: Harper & Row, 2001), 2.

label, as we will see with the others, we might call this view the "rejectionist" view. Christians are to reject the world in order to devote themselves to the love of God. The state of the world in which we live is such that Christians should extricate themselves from the institutions of society because those structures are inherently corrupt and sinful. Niebuhr rightly recognizes that this view is inadequate and naïve and that it mistakenly sees the world in extreme, moral, black-and-white terms. He lists Tertullian and some Christian monastics as examples. Still, he praises this view for its single-minded devotion to pursuing God.

Christ of Culture

The second model Niebuhr provides falls at the other end of the spectrum. If the "Christ against Culture" model refuses to accommodate to the morally complex realities of life, the "Christ of Culture" model goes too far in accommodating Christ to the world. This view sees no tension between the world and Christ, and in fact sees Christ as a culturally embedded teacher who taught religious truths for his day that cultures today might convey, though in different forms or religious systems. This view peers through Christ's particular teaching on sin, grace, and the Trinity to get at the core spiritual truth in his message. Adherents of this view then look for ways that their current culture teaches the same core truths.

Early gnostic heretics, as well as classic German Liberal theologians, embody this approach, according to Niebuhr. The stance of this view is a fundamental openness to the world, seeing every culture as a pathway to knowing God. Niebuhr rightly rejects this model as failing to hear the words of Christ for culture, for it places culture in the driver's seat for determining how Christians should live in society. As Niebuhr says, because of this there is very little that is truly Christian about this view, and it should be seen as beyond the bounds of historic Christianity.

Christ above Culture

The final three models that Niebuhr provides are similar in that together they represent the range of what the majority of Christians throughout history have adopted. Accordingly, all three views see culture as something that is natural to human life in creation and, therefore, in principle something that Christ does not stand against. Where the three differ, however, is in the overarching motifs of Christ's teachings on culture that each view sees as a paradigm for articulating how Christians should relate to culture.

The third model Niebuhr calls "Christ above Culture," and he describes it as the "synthesist" view which sees Christ teaching on two separate and seemingly unrelated topics: life in the world and the heavenly life of the spirit. For this view, both of these types of teachings on how to live concern different arenas of life, with the first organized by laws of reason while the second is organized by laws of religion. These are related by an "above" teaching on heavenly life that is superior and more sacred than the "below" teaching on secular life in the world.

Examples Niebuhr gives of this view are Thomas Aquinas and many of his Roman Catholic followers. In this view, there are two teachings from Christ that offer two different types of knowledge, and both are valid and important: one worldly and natural and the other heavenly and spiritual. While Christians should give priority to Christ's heavenly teaching on how to be saved, how the church is to gather for the sacraments, and other spiritual things, they should also "give to Caesar what is Caesar's" (Matt 22:21, paraphrased). That is, they should also validate the conclusions of culture that come from natural reason, like philosophy, civil governance and law, and science. But the way these things ought to be synthesized in the Christian life is that Christians should seek to be faithful in both arenas of life even as Christians set the higher spiritual life as the true goal and priority.

Christ and Culture in Paradox

The fourth of Niebuhr's models is "Christ and Culture in Paradox." In this view, Christ is understood to provide a pattern for the whole of our lives, which at the same time teaches us how to know him and be saved and to live faithfully in culture. Thus, Christ speaks both to our spiritual condition before God and to culture.

However, this view rejects any notion that Christ or Christian Scripture speaks in any way to what culture should be or should become at the hands of Christians in this life. Christ does not tell us how to practice medicine, form governments, or create art, only that we should do these things *Christianly*. Because of this, Niebuhr calls this view the "dualist" approach, and he gives Paul and Luther as examples. He argues that this view states that Christ has much to say to culture while, at the same time, stating Christ has nothing *directly* to say to culture at all. For those who hold this view, Niebuhr says they inhabit a paradox that ultimately cannot be resolved.

Christ the Transformer of Culture

The last of Niebuhr's models is the "Christ the Transformer of Culture" type, which he also calls the "transformationist" position (as well as "conversionist," on the basis that it aims to convert all culture into God-honoring culture). This model holds that sin is a misdirection of God's purposes for his creation and that Christ came not only to bring salvation but also to restore creation to what it was meant to be. Whereas the dualism of the paradox type tends to focus on the redemptive work of Christ from sin for personal salvation, for the transformationist, Christ's redemptive work is seen to apply to culture as well, which gives Christians an example to follow. Niebuhr cites Augustine as a preeminent example of this approach, for Augustine sees sin as pervasive throughout the whole person and therefore throughout all of culture; so the scope of Christ's redemptive work has not only the whole person in view but all of culture as well.

However, as Niebuhr warns, in practice transformationists find it difficult to hold consistently to seeing the need for Christ's salvation from sin and bringing all things under his rule as King over creation. This is true especially of nineteenth-century English socialist theologian F. D. Maurice, another example Niebuhr gives. Often, those who hold this view focus so much on transforming culture that they forget the reason culture needs transformation at all, namely that we are sinners in need of a savior.

NIEBUHR'S CHRIST AND CULTURE TYPOLOGY

Type	Description	Example
Christ against Culture (Rejectionists)	Christians should remove themselves from culture.	Tertullian
Christ of Culture (Universalists)	All culture can give knowledge of God.	Gnostics and Liberals
Christ above Culture (Synthesists)	Christ teaches on spiritual and earthly life, and spiritual life is a higher priority.	Aquinas
Christ and Culture in Paradox (Dualists)	Christ teaches on spiritual and earthly life, and Christians should hold these together in tension.	Paul and Luther
Christ the Transformer of Culture (Conversionists)	Christians should work to see all culture transformed by Christ.	Augustine and Maurice

Assessment

Niebuhr's typology shows us how Christians should relate to culture. In many ways he has set the terms of the discussion, and his is a classic work that anyone wanting to think deeply on this issue needs to interact with. However, his approach is not above critique. Several recent critics, like D. A. Carson and Craig Carter, rightly point out that when Niebuhr centers his models on how Christians think about Christ's cultural example, Niebuhr fails to take into consideration the whole scope of Scripture and the intricacies of God's purposes in his work of creation and salvation revealed throughout Scripture.[4] Certainly, Christ's life and teachings stand as the ultimate self-revelation of God in the flesh, and we should pay close attention to these. However, all of Scripture is God-breathed; and to rightly understand the words and actions of Christ, we need to read the parts in the relation to the whole. Niebuhr himself argues as much when he points out that each of these typologies do something different regarding culture when they focus on only certain aspects of Christ and his work. This, then, leads us to our next approach to describing the relationship between Christians and culture.

Herman Bavinck and the Nature and Grace Typology

If Troeltsch sees the conceptions of the church as paradigmatic for how to relate to culture and if Niebuhr sees conceptions of Christ as accounting for different stances, then the typology of nature and grace offers the way God relates to his creation as the lens through which to see things. While this approach has no one author, and both Augustine and Thomas Aquinas utilize these categories, the Dutch Neo-Calvinist tradition, especially

---

[4] See D. A. Carson, *Christ and Culture Revisited* (Grand Rapids: Eerdmans, 2008), 40–41; Craig A. Carter, *Rethinking Christ and Culture: A Post-Christendom Perspective* (Grand Rapids: Brazos, 2006), 68–69.

in the thought of Herman Bavinck, has uniquely leveraged these ideas as a cultural typology.[5]

In this paradigm, "nature" is shorthand for God's creation and all of his work in it concerning its original designs and purpose. "Grace" on the other hand refers specifically to God's work of addressing the problem interjected into the story of creation by sin and the fall.[6] Grace includes not only the work of Christ on the cross but also God's covenant with Abraham, his giving of the law to Israel at Sinai, and even God's words given as a written record in the Bible. This view asserts that how Christians understand the relationship between what God is doing with creation and what he made it for—and in what way and for what reason God is bringing redemption from sin—goes a long way toward explaining their various mindsets regarding culture.

Grace above Nature

The first model holds that the domains of nature and grace neatly separate into God's natural and supernatural work. Both are economies of God's activity in the world, but the relationship between these economies only goes in one direction. The realm of nature is the material world that, though good, is incomplete. If God's purpose for the world is for human beings to know and love him, then creation needs something added to it in order to

---

[5] Jan Veenhof, *Nature and Grace in Herman Bavinck*, trans. Albert M. Wolters (Sioux Center, IA: Dordt College, 2006).

[6] For a helpful summary of the views in this typology, see Bruce Riley Ashford and Craig G. Bartholomew, *The Doctrine of Creation: A Constructive Kuyperian Approach* (Downers Grove, IL: IVP Academic, 2020), 259–63.

elevate us into the proper spiritual state whereby we can know him, especially in a saving way in light of our fallen state. Thus, the realm of grace is understood as being of a higher, more complete, and purer reality that is infused into nature in order to transform it.

The quintessential example of this mindset is Roman Catholic sacramental theology, in which God's grace is understood to be a substance that infuses and transforms material things into a higher spiritual reality. This is like the transformation of the bread and wine of the Lord's Supper when they actually become Christ's body and blood in the Catholic mass in order to impart God's favor and forgiveness from sin. If this is the primary way of understanding how God relates to his creation, then the cultural attitude it can convey is one that prioritizes spiritual matters above earthly matters. Many Christians who then embrace this approach tend to focus on spiritual or church matters, like worship, the sacraments, or prayer, as being of greater importance than any other cultural forms. This, in turn, can shift the focus off public life in one's cultural context and onto private life that takes place inside the walls of the church or prayer closet.

Grace Opposed to Nature

In the next model, grace is seen not as supplementing and elevating the realm of nature but as actually opposing it. This is because this view sees the effects of sin on the realm of nature to be so great that any participation in nature results in spiritual or ethical compromise with the impure world. Because nature is so ruined by sin, this has given rise to God's new work of grace, which acts to undo the effects of sin in the realm of nature by calling Christians out of it. First, grace calls Christians to focus on the spiritual realities of redemption while one remains in this life. Then, Christians have the hope of death by which they will be liberated from this fallen world once and for all.

The monastics of the early church fled the polluting influence of society to spend their lives in quiet contemplation of spiritual matters as they awaited their final release from this worldly sojourn. After the sixteenth-century Protestant Reformation, some radical Anabaptists also embraced this framework based on literal interpretations of the passages in Scripture that warn about capitulation to the world. Some contemporary fundamentalists may also be influenced by this mindset today. The stance toward culture that it produces is one in which Christians must protect themselves from any culture that is not directly influenced by Scripture or is disconnected from the spiritual matters of grace and forgiveness. Thus, this posture flirts with an unchristian Gnosticism that sees God's creation as not very good at all.

Grace alongside Nature

If the first model holds that grace and nature are two realms that are fundamentally good, even if one is lower and incomplete, the model of grace alongside nature flips this arrangement on its side to hold that grace and nature are two equal domains of God's work and are autonomous and self-contained. The realm of nature does not need grace to elevate it in order to convey Christians to some higher state of being. Rather, grace and nature exist alongside one another and are two different arenas of the Christian life that are each ruled by Christ in different ways. The realm of nature consists of earthly life in all its social, political, economic, and vocational realities; and Christ rules over it by the moral law he has written into the very fabric of creation. Just as there are physical laws ordering the natural world, so human life in the realm of nature also is ordered by reason and the universal sense of right and wrong written on every human heart.

For this model, Scripture certainly reveals the existence of the self-sufficient realm of nature, but it does not have all that much to say about life in this realm. Rather, because Scripture mostly concerns God's work of bringing spiritual redemption from sin, the Bible addresses primarily the realm of grace. In this understanding, grace is the domain of faith, of trusting in Christ's atonement and being filled with the Spirit to live virtuously within the realm of nature.

Examples of this mindset include the Lutheran tradition, with its language of Christ's two kingdoms, which stresses that the church is given to order the spiritual life of grace and that the state and society are given by God to order all other arenas of culture. This results in a stance toward culture in which so-called secular vocations and cultural activities are good and natural for Christians to participate in, but they are not in the scope of the mission of the church. Therefore, Christians should be careful to keep these two domains of life separate, but in so doing, they often have difficulty perceiving how Scripture speaks to their everyday lives outside the walls of the church.

Grace Infuses and Restores Nature

Like the previous model, Grace alongside Nature, this model sees the realms of God's grace and nature as not hierarchically ordered. God's work of grace is not somehow above and on a higher spiritual plane and therefore more important than his work in the domain of nature. However, this view does see God's work of grace intersecting with the realm of nature, with grace infusing and restoring nature where sin has disordered it. According to this view, sin has not only resulted in guilt before God but also in a misdirection of all culture. Because God's work of grace has all of sin's effects in view, the reality of Christ's atonement, resurrection, and filling Christians with his Spirit has a direct effect upon all that sin has touched. This view sees it as part of the Christian mission in life to ensure that individuals come to saving knowledge of God and that all of culture is realigned to its proper function of glorifying God.

Because grace therefore infuses and restores nature, Scripture speaks not only to our spiritual state but also to the entirety of our lives in the world. Even if Scripture does not tell us specifically how to be doctors, lawyers, mechanics, or politicians, it does cast a vision for what these domains of culture are supposed to be oriented toward, and it calls Christians into those domains to be part of the redemption and restoration of culture—to walk wisely in God's world. The "Grace Infuses and Restores Nature" model is most associated with the Dutch Neo-Calvinist tradition from which this paradigm of nature and grace finds its origin. Figures such as Abraham Kuyper and Herman Bavinck have helped to popularize it, and it now figures prominently among many culturally conscious evangelical Christians.

Despite its compelling vision for a more intimate integration between faith and culture, the trajectory of this model deserves some careful evaluation. One weakness this view is susceptible to is a tendency to see all of human cultural life as equally the focus of the Christian calling and mission. Often the emphasis of this view can be placed on creating culture, especially engaging the sphere of politics, to the neglect of the prophetic task of preaching the gospel and the need to stand against the surrounding cultural trends at times.

BAVINCK'S NATURE AND GRACE TYPOLOGY

Type	Description	Example
Grace above Nature	Spiritual matters are superior to earthly life.	Some Roman Catholics
Grace Opposed to Nature	Sin has so wrecked the creation that Christians are called out of the world.	Radical Anabaptists
Grace alongside Nature	There are two domains and priorities of the Christian life held in tension.	Lutherans
Grace Infuses and Restores Nature	God's work of restoration impels Christians into the world.	Dutch Neo-Calvinists

Assessment

What sets the "Nature and Grace" typology apart from the other two is that this view is focused on how God relates to his creation and what he is doing in history. One's cultural attitude should be framed by the unified story of God's works of creation and redemption. This view holds that God's economies of nature and grace are two parts of the story of history that intersect directly with culture and that—if you hold them apart, close together, or in a hierarchy—you will understand humanity's relation to culture accordingly.

Because this typological approach rightly focuses on twin themes of creation and salvation, it offers a more compelling explanation of why Christians have differed so much on the issue of how to engage culture. As we argued in chapter 1, how we understand the whole story of Scripture and locate ourselves within it is central to understanding the way of Christ for cultural life. The "Grace Infuses and Restores Nature" model best captures the dynamic of how God's works of creation and salvation intersect, and it subsequently informs how we should live in response.

To show why this is, we turn in the next two chapters to look at God's design for how humanity is to relate to him and his creation and how Scripture provides the way of wisdom for us to follow throughout every area of life.

4

Creator and Creatures

We have no home in this world, I used to say,
and then I'd walk back up the road to this old
place and make myself a pot of coffee and
a fried-egg sandwich and listen to the radio,
when I got one, in the dark as often as not.
                        —Marilynne Robinson, *Gilead*

May God be gracious to us and bless us;
may he make his face shine upon us . . .
so that your way may be known on earth,
your salvation among all nations.
                        —Psalm 67:1–2

The opening quote from Marilynne Robinson's *Gilead* vividly captures the spirit of this chapter. It is eerily familiar to Western evangelicals who have been taught the "this world is not my home" and "we're just passing through" sort of doctrine. Certainly, the current way of the world is not the new heavens and earth that we long for, but the story of Scripture is not that God's creation is merely a first draft waiting to be discarded to the trash can and created *ex nihilo* all over again. Rather, we anticipate a coming purification of the current ways of the world, a realigning of the created order to the way of the Lord. And Peter tells us that this purification will occur as if by fire (2 Pet 3:10) as part of the events of that blessed-yet-dreadful day of the Lord long foretold by the prophets.

How then must we understand God and the world? How do we understand ourselves and our place in God's world? In chapter 2 we defined culture as "the ways and products of creatures in creation." In chapter 3 we considered how the church has related to culture historically and the models that have emerged as a result. In this chapter, we consider the doctrinal building blocks that frame our approach. The previous chapters have attended to the horizontal description of the story of Scripture and story of the church in relation to culture. Now we consider the doctrinal foundations that prop up the story and shore up the foundations of our approach. Specifically, we attend to our understanding of God the Creator, his relationship to the creation, who we are as imagers in creation, the role of the incarnate Son as the new Adam, and how all of this informs our purpose in the world.

Our Triune God

Of the many things we might say about who God is for our purposes in this volume we will limit ourselves to the following: *God is the triune Creator who is actively restoring all things to himself through the work of the Son by the power of the Spirit.* To begin, we must be clear that God is beyond our ability to explain or comprehend. By definition, God is beyond human capacity. As Isaiah reminds us, "For as heaven is higher than earth, so my ways are higher than your ways, and my thoughts than your thoughts" (Isa 55:9).

Furthermore, we are mindful of Eccl 5:2 as we approach God: "Do not be hasty to speak, and do not be impulsive to make a speech before God. God is in heaven and you are on earth, so let your words be few." Thus, speaking about the true and living God must be done humbly, thoughtfully, and *in accord with what he has told us about himself in Scripture.* We learn more about God with each turning page of the biblical story. While neither he nor his character changes (Mal 3:6), the entire story from Genesis to Revelation is necessary for a full picture of who God is.

Throughout Scripture, God is revealed as Father, Son, and Holy Spirit. This is a basic and historic Christian confession affirmed by the church since the time of the apostles and further clarified through the tradition of the early councils and creeds, including the Apostles' Creed:

> I believe in *God, the Father* almighty,
>   *maker* of heaven and earth.
> And in *Jesus Christ, his only Son, our Lord,*
>   who was conceived by the Holy Ghost,
>   born of the virgin Mary,
> suffered under Pontius Pilate,
>   was crucified, dead, and was buried;
>   he descended into hell.
> The third day he rose from the dead.
> He ascended into heaven

and [is seated at] the right hand of God the Father
almighty.
From [there] he shall come to judge the [living] and
the dead.
I believe in the *Holy Ghost,*
    the holy catholic* church,
    the communion of saints,
    the forgiveness of sins,
    the resurrection of the body,
    and the life everlasting.[1]

* "Catholic" here refers to the church universal.

The Bible employs many names for God. *Elohim* and *Yahweh,* for
example, are common Hebrew titles used in the Old Testament,
with *Yahweh* understood as the most proper and holy name of
God (see Exod 3:15 HCSB). But the most significant, theo-
logically and historically, are the names Father, Son, and Holy
Spirit. These three comprise what Christians refer to as the
Holy Trinity, the term used to capture both God's Oneness and
Threeness as revealed in Scripture.

God the Father

The name "Father" appears first in the baptismal formula of
Matt 28:19 and is commonly first in historic creeds and confes-
sions. We may understand God as Father in at least three ways.

---

[1] The Apostles' Creed, in Philip Schaff, *Creeds of Christendom,
with a History and Critical Notes,* 6th ed., vol. 1, *The History of the
Creeds,* Christian Classics Ethereal Library (Harper & Bros, 1877;
Grand Rapids: Baker), https://www.ccel.org/ccel/schaff/creeds1.iv.ii
.html. Italics added and certain words bracketed for clarity.

First, God is Father in the sense that he has a Son. The title "Father" thus expresses his relationship to his Son in a way that parents and children might understand to some degree. But there is also a deeper, mysterious sense that both Father and Son are uncreated and from eternity. We must also recognize that the names of Father, Son, and Spirit identify something distinctive about each Person while maintaining God's Oneness (Deut 6:4).[2] Second, God is Father in that he is the originator of all things. This applies to the Father as Creator (Maker) of heaven and earth, but it uniquely applies to the Father's grand plan, which orders all things according to his will and wisdom (see Rom 8:28; Eph 1:3–14) and is carried out by the Son, the Spirit, and the people of God. Third, God is the Father of his people. This is first understood as God as Father of the Israelites, the children of Abraham (Deut 32:6). As the story continues, he is understood as the Father of all who believe and obey the Son (Matt 5:45; Rom 8:15).

---

[2] See Herman Bavinck's discussion in *Reformed Dogmatics: Volume 2: God and Creation*, ed. John Bolt, trans. John Vriend (Grand Rapids: Baker Academic, 2004), 147. Bavinck writes, "The name is now the common name of God in the New Testament. The name YHWH is inadequately conveyed by Lord (χυριος) and is, as it were, supplemented by the name 'Father.' This name is the supreme revelation of God. God is not only the Creator, the Almighty, the Faithful One, the King and Lord; he is also the Father of his people. The theocratic kingdom known in Israel passes into a kingdom of the Father who is in heaven. Its subjects are at the same time children; its citizens are members of the family. Both law and love, the state and the family, are completely realized in the New Testament relation of God to his people."

God the Son—Jesus

As the story continues, the prophets promise the coming of One who will sit on David's throne forever, One who is more faithful than Abraham and greater than Moses, One who is "God with us," and One who will reign with justice and equity. Jesus of Nazareth was born in the small town of Bethlehem to the virgin Mary in approximately 4 BC during the reign of Caesar Augustus while Quirinius was governing Syria (Luke 2:1–2). As Matthew and Luke demonstrate, Jesus's lineage traces back to David through both Mary and Joseph, despite Joseph's having no physical part in Jesus's birth. Jesus's historic birth is one of many ways that the New Testament emphasizes his genuine humanity. But Scripture also presents Jesus as more than merely human. He is God in the flesh.

Four New Testament passages served as Christ hymns for early Christians, teaching them about Jesus in lyrical language. These include John 1:1–4; Phil 2:5–11; Col 1:15–20; and Heb 1:1–3. Countless volumes have been written on the riches of these passages, but for our purposes we briefly list the following:

- The Son existed "in the beginning" prior to creation as the eternal Word (*Logos*) of God.
- He is the "firstborn" (preeminent One) over all creation.
- All things visible and invisible were created through him and for him.
- All things hold together because of him.
- Life exists in him.
- He is the image (*icon*) of the invisible God.
- He is the exact expression of God's nature.
- He is equal with God.

- He, the Word, became flesh and dwelt among the people of the earth.

- He obeyed the Father by coming to earth as a man, dying for sinners, and rising from the dead.

- He is worthy of worship, and one day all will confess him as Lord to the glory of God the Father.

- He is the heir of all things and dwells now at the right hand of the Majesty on high.

In the mid-fifth century, bishops and pastors gathered from all over the known world to offer a definition of Jesus that was faithful to the Bible's testimony about him. This became known as the "Chalcedonian Definition of Christ," and it remains an important and authoritative articulation of Jesus's identity today.[3]

---

[3] The Definition of Chalcedon (451) reads as follows (emphasis added, though some italicized portions are in full caps in Bettenson and Maunder): "Therefore, following the holy Fathers, we all with one accord teach men to acknowledge one and the same Son, our Lord Jesus Christ, at once *complete in Godhead and complete in manhood, truly God and truly man, consisting also of a reasonable soul and body; of one substance with the Father as regards his Godhead, and at the same time of one substance with us as regards his manhood*; like us in all respects, apart from sin; as regards his Godhead, *begotten of the Father before the ages, but yet as regards his manhood begotten, for us men and for our salvation, of Mary the Virgin*, the God-bearer; one and the same Christ, Son, Lord, Only-begotten, recognized *in two natures, without confusion, without change, without division, without separation*; the distinction of natures being in no way annulled by the union, but rather the characteristics of each nature being preserved and coming together to form one person and subsistence, not as parted or separated into two persons, but one and the same Son and Only-begotten God the Word, Lord Jesus Christ; even as the prophets from earliest times spoke of him, and our Lord Jesus Christ himself taught us,

Jesus's incarnation remains a great and beautiful mystery for Christians, one that we do well to reflect upon daily. Moreover, we recognize Jesus's life and work as the apex of God's ongoing story of restoring all things to Himself through Christ.

God the Spirit

The Holy Spirit is often referred to as the third person of the Godhead. But this must in no way relegate the Spirit as lesser than the Father or Son. Rather, this simply follows the traditional expression given by Jesus in Matt 28:19 when he instructed his disciples to baptize "in the name of the Father and of the Son and of the Holy Spirit." The Spirit of God thus maintains his own identity (person) in the Godhead, though he is also understood to be God himself. In the fateful story of Ananias and Sapphira, both died immediately upon lying to the Holy Spirit. As Peter insisted, lying to the Spirit was lying to God (Acts 5:4).

Moreover, the logic and certainty of our salvation depends upon the distinct work of the Spirit *sealing* us for God's purposes, *empowering* us for holy living, and *sanctifying* us through belief in the truth of God (Romans 8; Eph 1:3–14; 2 Thess 2:13–14). The Spirit is the One who conceived Jesus in the womb of Mary, descended upon Jesus at baptism, led Jesus into the wilderness to be tempted, raised Jesus from the dead, then was sent by Jesus to glorify the Son and enable God's people to fulfill God's plan.

The God of the Bible thus reveals himself as the one true and living God as Father, Son, and Spirit. To truly know this

---

and the creed of the Fathers has handed down to us." Taken from H. Bettenson and C. Maunder, *Documents of the Christian Church*, 4th ed. (Oxford: Oxford University, 2011), 54–55.

God is to *know the Father through believing in the death and resurrection of the Son and by the indwelling presence of the Spirit.* For this is how we walk, worship, and pray. Perhaps the best and most historically faithful articulation of God's Triunity is found in the Nicene Creed:

> I believe in one God, the Father Almighty, Maker of heaven and earth, and of all things visible and invisible. And in one Lord Jesus Christ, the only-begotten Son of God, begotten of the Father before all worlds; God of God, Light of Light, very God of very God; begotten, not made, being of one substance with the Father, by whom all things were made. Who, for us men for our salvation, came down from heaven, and was incarnate by the Holy Spirit of the virgin Mary, and was made man; and was crucified also for us under Pontius Pilate; He suffered and was buried; and the third day He rose again, according to the Scriptures; and ascended into heaven, and sits on the right hand of the Father; and He shall come again, with glory, to judge the quick and the dead; whose kingdom shall have no end.
>
> And I believe in the Holy Ghost, the Lord and Giver of Life; who proceeds from the Father [and the Son]; who with the Father and the Son together is worshipped and glorified; who spoke by the prophets.
>
> And I believe one holy catholic and apostolic Church. I acknowledge one baptism for the remission of sins; and I look for the resurrection of the dead, and the life of the world to come. Amen.[4]

---

[4] "Nicene Creed," Christian Classics Ethereal Library, accessed September 19, 2023, https://www.ccel.org/creeds/nicene.creed.html.

Both the Apostles' and Nicene Creeds teach us that God is the "Maker [or Creator] of heaven and earth." This is a basic confession of our faith, and it is essential for careful consideration of Christianity and culture. The relationship between Creator and creation/creature is an essential link in the conversation about Christianity and culture. That God has created and maintained a relationship with creation despite rebellion and sin by his imagers speaks of his remarkable faithfulness and love for the creation. Furthermore, the creation itself is a window into the character of God—what Herman Bavinck refers to as an "ectype"—a sacramental reality that reflects the unity and diversity, creativity and wisdom, immanence and transcendence of our Lord. Finally, creation serves as the cultured environment in which the Son became flesh and ultimately restored the way of humanity's true nature in the world. This was followed by his sending of the Spirit that fills and directs God's people in the way and that will ultimately see God's plan brought to completion in a renewed heaven and earth.

God and Culture

If culture is the "ways and products of creatures in creation," we must evaluate God's relationship to culture as a comparison of *his* ways with the ways of any given culture. Let's begin with the following four assertions. First, God is active in this world. This may seem obvious, but sadly it is not assumed by all. For Christians, the very gospel we celebrate is predicated on the *missio Dei* (the mission of God)—that through the life, death, burial, and resurrection of Jesus—people can be born again of God's Spirit, rescued from sin, and enjoy the promise of life eternal with God. The second assertion is that the work of Jesus matters for the here and now of *this* world. This gospel is not some distant promise for a parallel universe or for a merely spiritual, heavenly reality. Jesus lived, died, and rose in *this* creation, this time and space dimension, and it is *this* creation in which God is still at work reconciling all things to himself.

Third, God's work is accomplished through the power of the Spirit. The same Spirit that raised Jesus from the dead is now at work in the people of God known as the church. God's purpose to restore all things through Christ will happen by the Spirit's filling and empowering men and women of God around the world to advance the ways of the King in his kingdom, beginning with the proclamation of the gospel. Fourth, in addition to God's activity in *this* world, we must also underscore God's activity in history. The economy of time and space that makes up our world serves as the suitable and necessary environment for the incarnation of the Son, which is, as Bavinck states, the "heart of history"[5]—that is all of time and space. Bavinck further urges, "The incarnation . . . has its presupposition and preparation in the creation . . . the creation of humans in God's image is a supposition and preparation for the incarnation of God."[6] All of this is to say that the

---

[5] H. Bavinck, *The Philosophy of Revelation: A New Annotated Edition*, ed. Nathaniel Gray Sutanto and Cory Brock (Peabody, MA: Hendrickson, 2018), 115.

[6] H. Bavinck, *Reformed Dogmatics*, vol. 3, *Sin and Salvation in Christ*, ed. John Bolt, trans. John Vriend (Grand Rapids: Baker Academic, 2006), 277.

"heart of history" is God with us, Christ in the flesh, for the renewal of his image in his people.[7]

Creatures in Creation: The Human Structure and Purpose of the Human Being

What does it mean to be human? Arguably this is the most pressing theological question of our day, as great confusion persists about the definition of a person, the nature of the self, gender, sexuality, human limitations, the integration of technology into the human body, and much more. For our purposes, we offer a basic outline of the structure, nature, and purpose of the human being.

Structure

Fundamentally, we hold that a human being is both a human body and a human soul, the whole of which is made in the image of God (*imago Dei*) for the purpose of glorifying God on earth. Further, by virtue of new birth in Christ by the Spirit, such persons are in the process of being remade into the image of Christ, *imago Christi* (2 Cor 3:18), which will be fully realized in the future glorification. Until then, in this life, Spirit-filled believers are called to image Christ in the world as citizens of his kingdom, to be salt and light, in word and deed. The degree

---

[7] For an excellent discussion of this, see the section titled "Christ Plays in History," in Eugene Peterson, *Christ Plays in Ten Thousand Places: A Conversation in Spiritual Theology* (Grand Rapids: Eerdmans, 2005), 131–222.

to which we do this properly is the degree to which we walk wisely in the world.

Both body and soul are essential components of the overall human constitution wherein the soul animates the body in a deeply integrated fashion. In this view, the soul carries the "blueprint" for the body and determines the uniqueness of each person, including gender.[8] Both body and soul contain faculties that manifest in the person through bodily activities, emotional dispositions, personality, athleticism, creative ability, intellectual strength, and so on. We do not claim to offer an exhaustive list of faculties here; rather, we simply aim to outline the broad strokes of the structure of humans.

Bodily faculties may include the senses of taste, touch, smell, sight, and hearing as well as the various systems of the body that are integral for proper bodily health. Of course, these are not divorced from the soul, as the eye requires not only the brain but the reality of consciousness to interpret and reflect

---

[8] We are sympathetic to the hylomorphist view of the human person as articulated by Jason Eberl, Eleanore Stump, David Oderberg, Ross Inman, and James K. Dew. While fine distinctions exist between those in the hylomorphist camp, the general Thomistic articulation of the combination of a rational (human) soul informing prime matter giving rise to a human being, and both the rational soul and prime matter (material body) being essential for the recognition of a full human person, is the view we affirm. Countless "what abouts" abound concerning the intermediate state, the nature of consciousness, the grounding of human elements such as race and ethnicity, the ground and origin of the soul, the federal versus natural headship of Christ, and so on. All are important matters that are beyond the scope of this work. Additional authors whose works we appreciate and readers may find valuable include Marc Cortez, J. P. Moreland, John Behr, Anthony Hoekema, Joshua Farris, David H. Kelsey, Richard Swinburne, Alvin Plantinga, and James K. A. Smith.

on what is seen. The precise relationship of body and soul to explain such things is highly debated and beyond our scope here. Faculties of the soul are more ambiguous as they defy our ability to observe and evaluate in any modern scientific way. Historically, however, Christians have identified at least the mind, will, and emotions as core faculties of the soul. In recent decades scholars have produced a mountain of literature debating the nature of the human person. Our aim here is not to sort through the literature nor to affirm a specific view on the many questions that abound in the conversation. Rather, we seek to offer the following thoughts as they relate to the Christian's posture and approach to culture.

First, by understanding ourselves as body and soul, with the soul acting to animate the body, our approach to proper Christian living in the world must go beyond mere *obedience in the body*. If the soul animates the body, the cultivation of virtue in the soul is essential for proper habit-formation in the body that leads to "walking wisely" in God's world. A volume such as the present one hovers on the threshold of the discipline traditionally referred to as Christian ethics. However, we stop short of treading upon this discipline whose first concern is final action (deontology) of the person. This is important and related, certainly, but our first concern is the posture and approach of the person, the congruence of body and soul in relation to our view (fear) of God and our view of creation as we seek to walk in his ways in the world.[9] Second, building on the

---

[9] This is not to suggest that Christian ethicists are merely concerned with action versus virtue. Rather, this is simply to clarify that our first concern is *posture and approach* that lead to wise walking (proper direction and wise action) in particular times and places.

point above, proper Christian care for self must extend to both body and soul, not just one or the other. Christians of various traditions wax and wane in their emphasis on bodily health and exercise. In our own Baptist tradition, we have historically not stressed the importance of bodily exercise as part of one's over-all Christian discipline and are often chided for our poor health and obesity. Conversely, much evangelical discipleship stresses intellectual growth over emotional and volitional exercise. Other traditions, especially the more charismatic, stress the experiential and emotional dimensions of growth and exercise.

The point is that proper Christian discipline and self-care should attend to the whole person—body and soul and all the faculties associated therewith. The language of head, heart, and hands may be helpful here for getting at the whole of the person. Discipleship and catechetical models that fill the head but neglect the heart and hands may be good, but not complete or sufficient. Models that attend closely to the heart with intense meditative and confessional exercises as well may be good but incomplete. Evangelicals are particularly good at the active side of evangelism, mission, and community service (hands) but often weak in disciplines of the head and heart. The Great Commandment stresses the whole person as "heart, soul, mind, and strength," and the horizontal dimension of neighbor-love pivots on "as yourself." In other words, we are called to love God

---

Regarding Christian ethics, we have high regard for those in the evangelical tradition who have and continue to think carefully about the manifold ethical issues of our day, such as Oliver O'Donovan, Dennis P. Hollinger, C. Ben Mitchell, J. Daryl Charles, Mark Liederbach, Andrew Walker, Jason Thacker, Ken Magnuson, and Scott B. Rae to name but a few.

with all of our selves, and we can only love our whole neighbor to the degree that we properly love our whole self.[10] As Irenaeus of Lyons aptly said concerning the person who is fully alive to God, "For the glory of God is the living man, and the life of man is the vision of God."[11]

Purpose

As God's imagers, we are the crown of creation. Let us not become arrogant about this, however, for with pride of place comes the weight of responsibility. As we learned in chapter 1, we still bear the responsibility to "keep and cultivate" God's world. This begins with the confession that we are *creatures*, not the Creator. This places us ever in second position behind God and in the posture of submission to God's authority. *And this is very good!* This is part of what was so good at the end of the sixth creation day when the Lord beheld that what he had made was "very good" (Gen 1:31).

It was good because creature and Creator were ordered properly to one another. People knew their proper place as creatures, their proper limits as finite beings who are not endowed with the many "omnis" of God. God is omnipresent, omnipotent, omniscient, and much more even beyond our comprehension. People, however, are limited by design. And it is best when we recognize and rest in this truth. Indeed, the first act of disobedience in Genesis 3 was an attempt to be "like God,"

---

[10] Worthy of mention here is Dennis P. Hollinger's helpful little volume *Head, Heart and Hands: Bringing Together Christian Thought, Passion and Action*, (Downers Grove, IL: IVP, 2005).

[11] Robert Grant, *Irenaeus of Lyons* (Nashville: Routledge, 1997), 116.

that is, to be "omni" or "unlimited" like God. Additionally, we are to maintain a posture of humble submission. Sadly, talk of submission is too often relegated to sermons on marriage from Ephesians 5, where Paul tells women to submit to their husbands as unto the Lord. Submission is not just for wives. Submission is for everyone.

To be human is to be under authority. To be fully human is to admit it. Men especially struggle with this as they grow out of adolescence to adulthood. The prideful and rebellious spirit celebrated in the West loves to sing "A Country Boy Can Survive" at the top of his or her lungs as a way of sticking it to bosses, the police, government, or anyone else who might "tell me what to do." But we are fools to celebrate this. Christlikeness begins with "Not my will, but thine, be done" (Matt 26:39 KJV). With his own life, Jesus modeled submitting his human will to the Father.[12] With his words, he taught us daily to confess this in prayer. "Your kingdom come. Your will be done on earth as it is in heaven" (Matt 6:10). Moreover, in Gethsemane Christ prayed three times that the cup of suffering that was before him might pass from him. "Nevertheless," Jesus prayed, "not my will, but thine, be done" (Luke 22:42 KJV). This act of Jesus submitting his human will to the Father's, followed by Jesus's obedience unto death, has a renewing effect on our human will today. Jesus's laying down his human will as an act of obedience to the Father

---

[12] This is not to affirm the wrongheaded notion of "Eternal Subordination of the Son" that has held many captive of late in evangelicalism. See Michael F. Bird and Scott Harrower, eds., *Trinity without Hierarchy: Reclaiming Nicene Orthodoxy in Evangelical Theology* (Grand Rapids: Kregel Academic, 2019).

was a necessary part of his passion leading to his crucifixion then his resurrection, securing his authority over sin and death and making possible our freedom from sin and enslavement to Christ—which is freedom.

A second feature of imaging Christ in the world is our responsibility to create culture. Perhaps this brings to mind the "creatives" of our day involved in areas such as the arts, technological development, engineering solutions for anything from hunger to sanitation, or authors that popularize imaginative places like Hogwarts, Narnia, or Gotham. Certainly, each of these represent arenas (or spheres) in which God's people are called to be active. But, more basically, the call to create is the advancing of God's ways in the world. Whether inventing sustainable energy solutions, writing the next bestseller, framing a house, coaching the baseball team, or preparing the evening family meal, God's charge to "keep and cultivate" by loving God and neighbor until Christ returns remains the daily marching orders for Christians of every time and place. But we must not stop at the "what" and "why" of creatures in creation—we must consider the "how."

People and Culture

So how *ought* we relate to culture? Psalm 67:1–2 reads, "May God be gracious to us and bless us; may he make his face shine upon us . . . that your way may be known on earth, your salvation among all nations." *Our responsibility in culture is to make known God's way on earth, and his salvation among all nations.* The psalmist begins the psalm by entreating the Lord's blessing and favor. For God to "make his face shine upon us" is the request for God to smile on his people. But why? Verse 2 answers the why: "so that your way may be known on earth, and your salvation among all nations."

First, we seek God's favor so that his ways may be known in his world. How do we do this? By walking faithfully with God in every time and place. Yes, *every* time and place. As Abraham Kuyper famously said, "There is not a square inch in the whole domain of our human existence over which Christ, who is sovereign over *all*, does not cry: 'Mine!'"[13] Indeed, Christ's authority does lay claim to every space and place in creation. Not just space, but time as well. Thus, we might add to Kuyper's comment that there's not one millisecond on the whole of the calendar where Christ has not made an appointment.[14]

Walking with God is an every-moment, in-every-place, inside-out kind of life. We must not merely spiritualize the point here. Walking is the great mega-metaphor in Scripture for how to live. It *literally* applies to all of life in body and soul. To make God's ways known on earth is not accomplished merely through prayer and spiritual disciplines. This is only the beginning. It is seen in dads who remain faithful to their wives and are patient with their kids, in coffee shop owners who serve excellent coffee at a fair price with joyful hearts, in geometry teachers who skillfully and creatively instruct future carpenters in the wisdom of the Pythagorean theorem in order to build

---

[13] Abraham Kuyper, "Sphere Sovereignty," in *Abraham Kuyper: A Centennial Reader*, ed. James D. Bratt (Grand Rapids: Eerdmans, 1998), 461.

[14] See Benjamin T. Quinn and Walter R. Strickland II, *Every Waking Hour: An Introduction to Work and Vocation for Christians* (Bellingham, WA: Lexham, 2016).

strong and long-lasting rafters, in the baseball coach who not only teaches the skills and strategy of the game but prepares boys for manhood and responsibility through the lessons of the game, in the marketing executive who inspires consumers to consider their needs and not just their wants when developing a new campaign, in the elderly widow entering her forty-third year of volunteering with the children at church. And so much more. Our bodies are instruments for virtue with which we must aim toward love for God and love for neighbor in every time and place. In so doing, by God's grace, we make known his way on earth.

Second, we seek God's favor so that the nations will know of his salvation. Often a dichotomy is forced between *living* for God and *evangelizing* about God. This is not an either/or; it is a both-and! Jesus left his disciples with the final instructions to "go . . . and make disciples" (Matt 28:18–20). Is this a call to evangelize the world? Certainly! But disciples are more than mouthpieces for the gospel. Disciples are bodies and souls formed into Christlikeness who strive to advance his ways in every time and place. The key is faithfulness. Faithfulness to Jesus includes both telling the world of the good news of Jesus *and* walking in his ways at home, at work, in our neighborhoods, at church, at play. This is the culture of Christ. This is at least a taste of the kingdom come on earth as it is in heaven.

Conclusion: Called to Walk Wisely

As creatures in God's creation, our purpose, our vocation, is to walk wisely in the world, at all times and in all places. As Paul wrote at the pivotal point of his letter to the Ephesians,

"Therefore I, the prisoner in the Lord, urge you to walk worthy of the calling you have received, with all humility and gentleness, with patience, bearing with one another in love, making every effort to keep the unity of the Spirit through the bond of peace" (Eph 4:1–3). But how exactly do we "walk wisely"?

5

Wisdom's Way

> Whenever I'm about to do something, I
> think, "Would an idiot do that?" And if
> they would, I do not do that thing.
> —Dwight Schrute, *The Office*

> Make your ways known to me,
> Lord; teach me your paths.
> —Psalm 25:4

> Though all the peoples walk in the name of
> their own gods, we will walk in the name
> of the Lord our God forever and ever.
> —Micah 4:5

Thus far we have overviewed the story of Bible (the *true story of the whole world*), offered a definition of culture and expanded on its meaning, surveyed approaches for how Christians have related to culture in the past, and considered both the significance of God as Creator and thus the author of culture as well as the significance for us as creatures embedded in cultures that emerge in creation. This chapter turns this book from *description* to *prescription*. Our fundamental proposal is that the biblical notion of "walking in the way of wisdom" is the best approach for cultural engagement. First, walking in wisdom accounts for God's ways in the whole of creation. Second, it considers the particularity of time and place, avoiding simplistic solutions to complex cultural realities; and third, it extends the already thick biblical metaphor of "walking in God's ways" into the everyday and ordinary, as well as extraordinary, areas of our lives and of culture.

In short, Christians are called to advance the ways of the King in the kingdom—in all of creation. A kingdom culture of love for God and neighbor necessarily results from kingdom citizens walking in the way of the King and advancing these ways in culture. Critical to consider, however, is, *How* ought Christians to go about this? Remembering the historical models considered in chapter 3, we affirm a "Grace Infuses and Restores Nature" view; and as Spirit-filled Christ-followers we approach all of life and creation on our toes, optimistic that while resistance will emerge in various times and places until Christ returns, there remains fundamental congruence between the ways of the King and the created order. And, as his imagers, we live under the authority of Christ the King, advancing his way in the world. The way of wisdom. The way of love. The way of Christ. This chapter will consider both "Why wisdom?" and "What is wisdom?" to grant clarity and concreteness to an otherwise nebulous idea. Finally, we will consider how wisdom intersects with and informs our view of creation, culture, and the church.

Why Wisdom?

The argument for the importance of wisdom in the Bible and for life needs no defense. But why such emphasis on wisdom for cultural engagement? We suggest the following five reasons. First, a wisdom approach centers on the person of Jesus. Paul, in 1 Cor 1:24, identified Christ as "the power of God and the wisdom of God." Further, in John 14:6, Jesus famously referred to himself as "the way, the truth, and the life." When considering how best to approach life in God's world, it is always right to look to Christ. And it must not be lost on us that the Scriptures identify Jesus, himself, as both Wisdom and Way.

Second, a wisdom approach connects the Bible's mega-metaphor of "walking in God's ways" to our consideration of cultural engagement. In the opening chapter, our overview of the biblical story accented the themes of "walking" and "way" throughout the Bible. But briefly consider Psalm 1 which begins, "How happy is the one who does not *walk* in the advice of the wicked or stand in the pathway with sinners or sit in the company of mockers!" (1:1) and ends, "*For the* LORD *watches over the way of the righteous, but the way of the wicked leads to ruin*"[1] (1:6). It is instructive for us that the first psalm, the introduction to the Hebrew hymnal, teaches God's people that there are two ways—and the Lord watches over the way of the righteous. It bears mentioning as well that the longest psalm in the Psalter, Psalm 119, is replete with *walking* and *way* language: "How happy are those whose way is blameless, who walk according to the LORD's instruction! Happy are those who keep

---

[1] Italics added for emphasis.

his decrees and seek him with all their heart. They do nothing wrong; they walk in his ways" (Ps 119:1–3). The end of
Psalm 1 reminds us also of the end of Jesus's Sermon on the
Mount in Matthew 7. He concludes his longest single teaching
in the Gospels with a comparison of two ways, one wise and
one foolish:

> Therefore, everyone who hears these words of mine
> and acts on them will be like a wise man who built his
> house on the rock. The rain fell, the rivers rose, and
> the winds blew and pounded that house. Yet it didn't
> collapse, because its foundation was on the rock. But
> everyone who hears these words of mine and doesn't
> act on them will be like a foolish man who built his
> house on the sand. The rain fell, the rivers rose, the
> winds blew and pounded that house, and it collapsed.
> It collapsed with a great crash. (vv. 24–27)

Third, "way," like "wisdom," is all-encompassing, a totality
concept to describe the whole of human behavior, both individual and communal.[2] Walking is a directional activity. It is
literally impossible not to walk in a particular direction, a particular *way*. As a metaphor that describes our manner of life,
the "way" in which we walk connects to the directional—that
is, *moral* or *meaningful*—nature of every aspect of life. Just as
it is impossible not to walk in a particular direction, it is also
impossible for any part of life to be neutral, without meaning or

---

[2] See Ray Van Leeuwen, "Wisdom Literature," in *Dictionary for
Theological Interpretation of the Bible*, ed. Kevin J. Vanhoozer (Grand
Rapids: Baker Academic, 2005), 848.

moral value. The key question, therefore, is, "Which way are we walking?" When we attend closely to this question as it relates to every area of our lives before God, we begin to hear just how loudly the Scriptures speak to the importance of walking in the way of the Lord, the way of Christ Jesus.

Fourth, "wisdom" is relevant for all people in every time and place. As wisdom is a totality concept, it is difficult to boil down to a definition. It also is not a one-size-fits-all idea. Wisdom adapts to the particulars of times, places, people, and circumstances. We will discuss this further below, but as part of our defense for "Why wisdom?" we want to stress that our cultural attitudes, postures, and approaches must attend carefully to particularity and avoid generalities, for wisdom adapts to such nuance and diversity.

Fifth, walking in a new and better way is accentuated in the Christian teaching of new birth. Ephesians 2:1–10 is particularly insightful here as in vv. 1–3 Paul described an old way of walking (manner of life) that was in accord with "the ways of this world . . . the ruler of the power of the air, the spirit now working in the disobedient." Then v. 4 pivots to describe a new *walk* that results from new birth. The passage ends with a "What now?" type of instruction for believers. The ESV more accurately accents the new way of walking as follows, "For we are his workmanship, created in Christ Jesus for good works, which God prepared beforehand, that we should *walk in them*."[3]

---

[3] Emphasis added.

So, What Is Wisdom?

I have never met a person who did not desire wisdom. Once on a plane a gentleman asked me what I was studying in school. I told him I was writing on the Christian doctrine of wisdom. He quickly informed me that he was not a religious person but that he was deeply interested in wisdom. I asked him how he would define wisdom, and after a pondering for a few minutes he remarked, "Doing things right."

He's not far off! While his answer may lack depth, the gentleman was getting at the heart of wisdom and illustrating the human desire to live rightly.

But what is wisdom? As in many other cultures and religions with wisdom traditions, wisdom is important to the Christian tradition. More than important, in fact—foundational. As mentioned above, wisdom defies definition. Thus, we offer the following essential components of wisdom that must be considered for a full understanding of biblical wisdom. We confess that there may be more essential components that should be included, but we would argue there cannot be less. We recognize these as essential and irreducible components of Christian wisdom according to the biblical witness.

First, wisdom is an attribute of the triune God, fully realized in the person of Jesus.[4] While the majority of our concern in this

---

[4] Further consideration of these can be found in Benjamin T. Quinn, *Walking in God's Wisdom: The Book of Proverbs* (Bellingham, WA: Lexham, 2021). Additionally, these are adapted from Craig Bartholomew and Ryan O'Dowd, *Old Testament Wisdom Literature: A Theological Introduction* (Downers Grove, IL: IVP Academic, 2011). Bartholomew and O'Dowd also cite Raymond Van Leeuwen as the originator of these "categories."

volume is the creaturely dimension of wisdom, we recognize that "wisdom" also properly describes the nature of God, who is Father, Son, and Spirit. As Augustine taught, wisdom (like love, justice, etc.) is not associated with only one person of the Godhead, but with all three.[5] Yet Paul stressed Christ, the Son, as the "power of God and the wisdom of God" (1 Cor 1:24), underscoring the importance of wisdom incarnate as the means by which the way of God's wisdom contrasts the wisdom of the world. This wisdom was reestablished in creation through the virgin birth, sinless life, atoning death, and victorious resurrection of Jesus.[6]

Second, wisdom begins in the fear of the Lord. Proverbs famously declares that the fear of the Lord is the beginning of both knowledge and wisdom (1:7; 9:10). This turns us directly to the creational dimension of wisdom. The fear of the Lord is our living confession of faith in the Maker of heaven and earth.[7] Living rightly, that is wisely, in God's world has a particular starting point—a proper view of the living God. In brief, wisdom in life begins not with ourselves, the wonder of the mountains, the ocean, the clouds, a certain response to human emotion,

---

[5] See Augustine, *The Trinity* (*De Trinitate*), 2nd ed., ed. Edmund Hill and John E. Rotelle (New York: New City, 2012), bk. 7, chap. 2.

[6] In *De Trinitate*, Augustine also identifies multiple dimensions of wisdom (*sapientia*) including the wisdom that is God (God's essence or nature) and created wisdom that is available to people. This is particularly the concern of *De Trinitate*, book 14, chapter 1, where he says, "God himself is supreme wisdom; but the worship of God is man's wisdom."

[7] Henri Blocher argues in his excellent article "The Fear of the Lord as the 'Principle' of Wisdom'" that the Old Testament notion of "fear of the Lord" and the New Testament notion of "faith" are basically synonymous. *Tyndale Bulletin* 28 (1977): 27.

reason, or intuition—it begins with the confession that the Lord is God and we are not. This confession establishes us in God through Christ and, by the Spirit the Lord, is our starting place and our *telos*, to know in the fullest sense God's mystery in Christ "in [whom] are hidden all the treasures of wisdom and knowledge" (Col 2:2–3).

Third, those who have wisdom seek to live in accord with creation. It should come as no surprise that if Wisdom made the world, signs of wisdom will be found in creation itself. Wisdom is woven into creation's ways, rhythms, and creatures; it is etched into its grooves and heard in the songs of nature. When correcting the lazy, the author of Proverbs points to the ant as a hardworking creature who gathers in summer in preparation for winter: "Go to the ant, you slacker! Observe its ways and become wise. Without leader, administrator, or ruler, it prepares its provisions in summer; it gathers its food during harvest" (6:6-8). Psalm 1 illustrates the "blessed" life as being like a tree planted by streams of water. The flourishing of the tree parallels the flourishing of the person who delights in the law of the Lord. Even the command to observe the sabbath is a rhythm of wisdom observed by the Creator himself and woven into the rhythm of his creatures. To work is basic to our human vocation, and to rest is basic to knowing the peace of God in Christ.

Fourth, wisdom adapts to particular circumstances. The general point here is twofold. First, wisdom is not one-size-fits-all. What is wise in one situation may not be wise in another. This is classically illustrated in the example from Prov 26:4–5: "Don't answer a fool according to his foolishness or you'll be like him yourself. Answer a fool according to his foolishness or he'll become wise in his own eyes." Is this a blatant contradiction in the Bible? An editorial oversight by the author of Proverbs? Not at all. This is an example of the nature of wisdom. Sometimes the wisest approach is to ignore the loud-mouthed, know-it-all. And other times, it is wise to correct the person and confront his foolishness. In such instances, we must discern if the person is teachable and willing to receive correction. If so, we do well to correct the fool. If we are confident that the person does not have ears to hear correction, we need not risk an argument with a fool and become like him in the process.

The second general point is that wisdom attends to specific times and places. The author of Ecclesiastes spoke of the importance of times and seasons when he wrote:

There is an occasion for everything,
and a time for every activity under heaven:
a time to give birth and a time to die;
a time to plant and a time to uproot;
a time to kill and a time to heal;
a time to tear down and a time to build;
a time to weep and a time to laugh;
a time to mourn and a time to dance;
a time to throw stones and a time to gather stones;
a time to embrace and a time to avoid embracing;
a time to search and a time to count as lost;
a time to keep and a time to throw away;
a time to tear and a time to sew;
a time to be silent and a time to speak;
a time to love and a time to hate;
a time for war and a time for peace. (Eccl 3:1–8)

Consider the goodness of a fire in the fireplace on a cold night. It warms the room and protects against dangerously cold temperatures. But both the time (a cold night) and the place (fireplace) are required for a wise application of building a fire. Move the fire to the middle of the bed (wrong place) or to a hot summer evening (wrong time), and the wisdom of building a fire is lost. It becomes foolish, even dangerous. Wisdom attends to both time and place.

Fifth, wisdom is rooted in tradition. One friend of mine (Benjamin's) is fond of saying that a family cookbook is wisdom, for it is a carefully curated index of culinary best practices. It's a multigenerational engagement with creation that fills the family table with creativity and familiar flavors that are celebrated and anticipated time and again. Such quality food is not produced the first time, but after years, even generations, of putting one's hands to the stuff of the earth and crafting delectable cuisine. So it is with wisdom.

The Proverbs are written in a parent-to-child, older-to-younger, apprenticeship-in-life form of teaching. What the parent seeks to give the child is not the recipe for grandma's stuffed turkey, but the recipe for how to live. Such knowledge is not acquired overnight, but after years, even generations, of engaging in life in the fear of the Lord and walking in Wisdom's way. Like a book of recipes, life lessons from parents to children, grandparents to grandchildren, may be handed down as not mere family tradition but as tradition that aligns with true wisdom.

Sixth, wisdom always corresponds to love for God and neighbor. When asked by the lawyer, "What is the greatest commandment?" Jesus straightforwardly answered with the great twin commands to love God and love neighbor, for "all the

Law and the Prophets depend on these two commands" (Matt 22:40). What is interesting about Jesus's answer is not only what he said but also what he did not say. He did not say the most important command is to read the Bible and pray. He did not say it was to share the gospel, engage in missionary activity, and support social justice advocacy. All of these are of great importance according to Scripture. But when Jesus was asked to boil it down to the "greatest commandment," he centered his answer on love that takes a cruciform shape—vertical love for God first and horizontal love for others second. And the order of these loves is as important as the commands themselves.

True wisdom always corresponds to the twin commands to love God and neighbor. In fact, we suggest that, as part of practicing biblical wisdom, we should cultivate the practice of asking the question, "What is the best expression of love for God and neighbor in this time and place?" According to Jesus's answer to the lawyer, this is always a good and right question, for it strikes at the very center of the most important matters of life before God. Wise decisions are not always obvious, not always black and white, right and wrong. If they were, we would not need wisdom, just the discipline to make the right decision. But in those moments of uncertainty, or when choosing between a good versus a best, considering the best expression of love for God and neighbor is a sure nudge toward advancing wisdom in the world.

Wisdom and Creation

Wisdom accounts for both what *is* and what *ought to be* in the world. Wisdom accounts for what *is* by virtue of being the agent of creation. The author of Proverbs wrote, "The LORD founded the earth by wisdom and established the heavens by understanding" (3:19). Not only is wisdom the agent of creation, but wisdom is also the *ought* of creation. In Proverbs 3 the author immediately moves from a point of ontology concerning creation to a point of morality and right living within the creation:

> Maintain sound wisdom and discretion.
> My son, don't lose sight of them.
> They will be life for you
> and adornment for your neck.
> Then you will go safely on your way;
> your foot will not stumble.
> When you lie down, you will not be afraid;
> you will lie down and your sleep will be pleasant.
> Don't fear sudden danger
> or the ruin of the wicked when it comes,
> for the LORD will be your confidence
> and will keep your foot from a snare. (3:21–26)

The move between the way creation *is* to the way creation *ought to be* is instructive for us. For creation—including people—*is* made by Wisdom and for God. Creatures, people in particular, are not autonomous and self-defining as contemporary culture may insist. Rather, the Bible is clear that God is the architect of all things and that by wisdom the world was founded. The *ought*, therefore, is to maintain wisdom and discretion, not losing sight of them, for "They will be life for you" (Prov 3:22). Few things in the Bible are described as having the power of life, but Wisdom is one of those. As the world was built by Wisdom, so should life be lived by wisdom. To live according to wisdom is to live according to the Creator's intention. Put another way, to live according to wisdom is to really live.

Wisdom and Culture

The *is* of creation, God's work, is accompanied by the *ought* of God's way. This is the *way* God's people are to *walk* in the world. This is the way of wisdom. As we've defined, culture is the ways and products of creatures in creation. These "ways and products" are necessary by-products of human interaction with creation. And ways and products are not neutral. They are laced with meaning, promoting a particular way or direction in God's world. Our task as Christians is to consider carefully which way is promoted by these cultural manifestations and to ensure that our ways and products intentionally promote the way of the Lord in creation.

Wisdom and the Church Today

As the family of God, God's children are called to be the salt and light of Christ and the wisdom of God in the world. Abraham Kuyper and Herman Bavinck spoke of the church both as an organism and as an institution.[8] As an organism, the people of God are sent into the world through their workplaces, families, communities, schools, and beyond—all cultural spheres—on mission to live the hope of Christ's gospel in word and deed.

---

[8] Cf. H. Bavinck, *Reformed Dogmatics: Abridged in One Volume*, ed. John Bolt (Grand Rapids: Baker Academics, 2011), 607–17.

While culture and community are forming, this approach of loving enemies and praying for persecutors may be dangerous and terribly inconvenient. Often this approach opposes the ways of particular cultures founded on values other than love for God and neighbor. As such, this approach is sometimes distinctly countercultural. The hope-filled, love-directed life is a life characterized by the fruit of the Spirit—love, joy, peace, patience, kindness, goodness, faithfulness, gentleness, and self-control—against which things there is no law. It is a way of life that is aimed at God and neighbor and is fundamentally *for* the world. This way of life is only possible when faith in Jesus produces the fear of the Lord that leads to loving obedience. Such is the beginning, means, and end of lived wisdom.

As an institution, the church gathers weekly to remember our "one Lord, one faith, one baptism" (Eph 4:5), celebrating the gospel of Jesus through corporate worship. As we practice baptism, partake in the Lord's Supper, confess our faith and our sin, pray together, preach the Scriptures, sing songs and hymns and spiritual songs to the Lord, and support the ministries of the church, we breed a particular culture, a culture of wisdom and community of wisdom in and for the world. Each component of corporate worship directs our attention toward God and the world, reminding us of our beginning in the Lord and of our purpose as lovers of God and others. Such weekly formation tills the soil of the human soul toward faithful, daily living in the body. This formation in Christ serves to correct the counter-formation of the world whose ways are opposed to the ways of the Lord. The ways of Christ and his people begin not with "me" and "mine" but with the confession that only God is God, that we are creatures fashioned in his image, and that as his people we are called to walk the way of wisdom in his world.

Conclusion

As we turn to the final chapters, we pull together the biblical, theological, historical, and contemporary threads to offer a framework for wise cultural engagement. Much of this is offered in the form of questions. This is intentional because questions offer a direction for consideration as opposed to answers that may not fit the time or place. Our aim is not to answer or anticipate every question one may have about a particular expression of cultural engagement. Rather, in keeping with a "Grace Infuses and Restores Nature" posture and the conviction that Christians are called to advance Christ's ways in the world, we offer a series of questions that we believe will assist God's people toward wise living and, therefore, wise cultural engagement.

6

The Questions We Ask: Part 1

The gospel calls us back again and again to the
real clue, the crucified and risen Jesus, so that we
learn the meaning of history is not immanent in
history itself, that history cannot find its meaning
at the end of a process of development, but that
history is given meaning by what God has done in
Jesus Christ and by what he has promised to do;
and that the true horizon is not at the successful
end of our projects but in his coming to reign.
—Lesslie Newbigin, *The Gospel in a Pluralist Society*

In this primer on cultural engagement, we offer a framework
for how to think about culture, using the very biblical metaphor of walking in the way of Christ as cultural creatures. The
first four chapters were mostly descriptive, exploring what culture is and how it fits in biblical narrative. In the previous chapter, we turned to offer something more prescriptive: if wisdom

concerns what God's creatures *ought* to do in God's creation, then the *ought* of walking in the way of wisdom presents us with a task. We are charged by God to pursue the ways of the King and his kingdom in every square inch and every waking hour of our lives—especially in our engagement with culture.

All of human life is cultural. This means that everywhere we find human culture, we find a path to walk. We either find a place where Jesus's kingdom has already come to earth, brought in by the cultural worlds of meaning we or Christians who have gone before us have created—think of the beautiful hymns Christians in faraway countries sing in their own languages, the jobs created for the homeless by an enterprising Christian businesswoman, or a bus shuttling weary pastors to a prayer retreat—or we find a place where Jesus's kingdom has yet to come: a complex vista of uncharted land which we must navigate.

Recall that as we consider the task of walking in the way of Christ, every potentially wise path is presented to us with an alternative, shadow path of folly. All things can be directed either unto the Lord or away from him. And even if we choose the path of wisdom, it does not just matter that we are directed toward the proper goal, but it also matters how we walk.

Our Map

In the final two chapters we bring together all the framework for cultural engagement we have developed together into a prescriptive vision for how to do cultural engagement properly unto Christ. However, what we aim to offer is not a one-size-fits-all model that tells you exactly what to do in every situation.

Rather, we offer a set of questions worth asking in any cultural context in which you find yourself. These form a sort of cartography of wise cultural engagement, a map with landmarks to be used to get our bearings. To recognize the landmarks and then know how to proceed toward the proper destination on the map, we need to ask the right questions.

Triangulation: Locating Ourselves on the Map of Culture

We have used the metaphor of Christians being presented with a way to walk in following Christ and advancing his kingdom in the world, and this way is always cultural. To answer *how* we are to walk this way, let us explore the related metaphor of wayfinding. When a sailor on the open ocean with a sextant in hand or a Boy Scout lost in the woods with only a map and compass seeks to answer the questions "Where am I? How do I get where I need to go?" their first task is to pull out a map.

Unlike a modern GPS, a map does not tell you where you are exactly, but only where particular landmarks are that you might be able to see on the horizon. For the sailor, this might be a lighthouse or some stars. For the Boy Scout, it might be a mountain or a lake. To figure out where they are on the map, they need to determine their position relative to fixed landmarks. This involves triangulation. If you can identify at least two landmarks and measure the angle from you to each of them based on some fixed reference point—such as a compass needle pointing north—then you can establish where you are. Once you know where you are, then you need to figure out where you are going and make a plan for how to get there.

Let us consider something similar when it comes to cultural engagement.

Orientation: When Are We?

The map that we have to help us in the task of walking in the way of Christ through culture is Scripture. But what is the nature of this map, and what does it tell us? As we have mentioned, Scripture is the written record of God's self-revelation to his creatures, inspired by the Holy Spirit and authoritative for knowing God and following his ways (2 Tim 3:16). Among many things, it tells us what God has said about himself, what he has done, and what he will do across history. In short, it tells the story of God and his dealings with his creation, *the true story of the whole world*. It is therefore no exaggeration to say that Scripture is *the* book of history. While many things that have happened in history are not mentioned in Scripture, it gives us the story of history from God's point of view. That is, it tells us exactly what he finds most important about creation, what has taken place in time, and what is to come.

God's Telling of History

This is important. The Bible is God's forthtelling of what has taken place that is truly meaningful for navigating life in his world, and it is a foretelling of where all of this is headed in light of this meaning. Unlike human accounts of history, the Bible presents an account that is accompanied by a divine explanation of what it is all about and how it all fits together. It is like having a script in which the screenwriter has provided all the notes in the margin about what is really happening in a scene and why it all matters for the plot of the film.

We see this every time Scripture explains what God is up to. For example, when Joseph was enslaved in Egypt because of the evil intent of his brothers, Joseph could see that "God meant it for good" (Gen 50:20b ESV). We see it also every time the people of Israel and their kings "did what was evil in the sight of the LORD" (Judg 2:11 ESV).[1] Their exile from the land, foretold in Deut 28:36–37, was not only judgment for their infidelity to God but also an opportunity for his great plan of rescue, when God would restore them with a new covenant (Jeremiah 31; Ezek 36:24–30) through the suffering of his servant (Isaiah 53), who will sit on David's throne forever (2 Sam 7:11b-16). This servant is Jesus Christ, God himself incarnate in human flesh: "For God who said, 'Let light shine out of darkness,' has shone in our hearts to give the light of the knowledge of God's glory in the face of Jesus Christ" (2 Cor 4:6).

The map of Scripture is God's story, not only telling us what has happened "long ago" but presenting us face-to-face with the divine Son, the heir of all things and through whom God made the universe, the one who is "the exact expression of [God's] nature" (Heb 1:1–3). He is the "image of the invisible God" (Col 1:15), the Word who was with God and who is God and who has revealed God to us (John 1:1, 18). The Christ event, when this "Word became flesh and dwelt among us" (John 1:14), is the great climax of history. To paraphrase Saint Augustine, all things

---

[1] This refrain appears throughout the books of 1 and 2 Kings, among many other places in Scripture.

triangulate from him, for he is the center and central meaning of history.[2]

When Are We?

Indeed, this map is strange. Instead of rivers, valleys, and lakes, its landscape is dotted with plot movements, thematic reveals, and climactic events. Instead of coming to it asking the question of "Where are we?" we ask the questions "When are we? What time is it? Where are we in the great story of God's redemption? What has happened, and what is yet to come?" We orient ourselves in life based on where we locate ourselves in God's telling of history.

Answering such "when" questions means we must attune closely to the narrative of Scripture. We need to know the story inside and out. This is easier said than done. For Scripture tells this story in many ways, sometimes zooming in to tell of God's covenant works with particular people, other times providing indictment against those peoples' sins or even our own sins. In other places, Scripture gives us words to pray and sing in our worship, instructions to live by as we make our way through the story, and even visions of the final end of history, which are scattered mysteriously throughout the various books of the Bible. Scripture does not always unfold the story in a linear, point A to point B, fashion.

---

[2] See his discussion of Christ's prefiguring in the prophecy of the Old Testament, which reveals Christ's annunciation as the great climax of history in Augustine, see Augustine, *The City of God*, ed. Boniface Ramsey, trans. William Babcock (New York: New City, 2013), bk 17.

A case in point is the already-not-yet of the kingdom: Jesus told his disciples that the kingdom was "at hand" (Matt 4:17 ESV), and yet he told them to pray expectantly that God's kingdom would come (Matt 6:10), and even that the kingdom was coming (Matt 26:29). This future-time kingdom, long prophesied throughout the Bible, was portrayed by Jesus himself as both having arrived and yet still a long way off. So answering the question, "When are we?" is not so straightforward.

Between the Times

Still, the major plot movements are clear enough, and they serve as landmarks by which to count time and determine our current location in the story. Recall that the story opens on the Creator making the world out of nothing. God set creation on its course and gave to humans, his imagers, a way in which to walk. This is a cultured path, a task to direct all things to God and his holy purposes. But humanity chooses another way, misdirecting all things away from God. Sin, death, and judgment entered the story, requiring God to rescue his imagers from the evil folly they have chosen. So God covenanted with a people, rescued them, and led them into a sacred land where they might show the world, as if on a stage, who the one true God is and how he is to be known and followed. However, God's people time and again walked another way, and their culture revealed their sin rather than their sacred Lord.

But God does not abandon his people or his plan for history. The great climax of the story comes with the arrival of Christ Jesus, the Son of God and true imager of him *par excellence*.

Jesus's arrival marks the beginning of the end of the story. His life of walking in God's true way, where Adam and Moses and all Israel failed, fulfilled God's purposes and promises given since the beginning (2 Cor 1:20). Even more, his death for us secures our atonement for sin, and his resurrection imparts life everlasting. Thus, with the arrival of Christ, the end of history has come near. Yet the story of Scripture is not quite done. Jesus foretold a final judgment in which all the work he began would be made complete, and he ascended to heaven with the promise that the gift of his Spirit would usher in the last days (Acts 2:17).

The filling of the Spirit in the hearts of God's people inaugurated a new age, a final time *between the times*. Located after the first and before the second coming of Christ, we find ourselves in a part of the story marked by great landmarks of Jesus's work revealed behind us and the full consummation of his work on the horizon ahead. We live in the age of the church, when Jesus sends his people out into the world to witness to what he has done and proclaim the hope of what he will do: "But you will receive power when the Holy Spirit has come on you, and you will be my witnesses in Jerusalem, in all Judea and Samaria, and to the ends of the earth" (Acts 1:8). As Newbigin puts it, "The meaning of the 'overlap of the ages' in which we live, the time between the coming of Christ and His coming again, is that it is the time given for the witness of the apostolic Church to the ends of the earth."[3]

---

[3] Lesslie Newbigin, *The Household of God: Lectures on the Nature of Church* (Eugene, OR: Wipf and Stock, 2008), 135.

Cultural Engagement in the Time in Between

As Scripture reveals that the story is now drawing to a close, the clues to when the end will finally be here are shrouded in mystery. Anyone who has ever read the book of Revelation can say amen to that. Christ himself precluded any speculation that the end has finally arrived (Matt 24:36), as if to say, "You will know it when you finally see it. Until then, it is not for you to know." But what we are given is very clear. In this time between the times, we possess a particular mission that provides us with a unique way to inhabit this time, with specific callings and purposes. Certainly, all that God has instructed about filling the earth with his image, walking in his ways, loving God and neighbor all still apply. Yet in this time, they apply in ways that ought to shift our priorities and focus our engagement with culture.

With the first coming of Christ, God's kingdom has arrived. In this age of the Spirit's filling, this kingdom unfolds across the whole earth as Christians walk in the ways of the King. And this involves so much more than just preaching words about who Jesus is, what he has done, and how to find salvation in him. Certainly, the predominant activity of Christians in this time in between is announcing the great epoch-shaping things that Christ has done in history and what they mean. This is the age of evangelism, of proclaiming the gospel until our King comes again. However, think about all the ways Jesus described what his kingdom is like: it's full of healing from disease and sickness (Matt 4:23; 9:35), those who inhabit it exhibit righteousness and humility (Matt 5:20; 13:43; 18:4), the kingdom is a treasure we should give anything for (Matt 13:44), and it is full of both the poor in spirit and those who are generous with their wealth (Matt 5:3; 19:23–24).

All of these descriptions in some way find cultural expression. If culture is the ways and products of creatures in God's creation, then the kingdom of God always finds expression through our culture. This expression is not merely or even most importantly in the sense that we literally build cities, thrones, and civilizations to see the kingdom on earth. Rather, it comes daily through the way we walk humbly in the way of the King in every cultural arena of our lives. As we have said, we are hard-pressed to find anything clearer concerning how to walk the way of Christ than Jesus's own summary of all God's instructions: "Love the Lord your God with all your heart, with all your soul, and with all your mind. This is the greatest and most important command. The second is like it: Love your neighbor as yourself" (Matt 22:37–39).

These commands to love God with all that we are and love our neighbors as our own selves are timeless. God called Israel to these same things in Deuteronomy 6. However, the ways in which Israel was meant to do this had some particular things in view. As we have mentioned, God called Israel to be his kingdom of priests who image him to the watching nations by the ways in which they were instructed to live in his land of promise, under God's commands for the whole of their lives. Additionally, when Israel was brought into exile, God instructed his people to seek the welfare of the city of their captors, living faithfully for him as they hoped for restoration (Jer 29:4–7).

Similarly, in this time in between the times, we have certain ways in which we are especially called to love God and our neighbors. We are to preach the good news of the gospel, leverage our resources and callings in service to this mission, and serve the church as it grows and spreads across the globe in its disciple-making advancement. We are to pursue the Spirit's work of fruit-fulness in our lives, producing the virtues of faith, hope, and love as we are formed into Christ's image. Certainly, all of these things can take place in every cultural arena of life. The farmer might grow food for his family and his community, and through this he might love God and neighbor well. The accountant may support fiscal responsibility and ethical transparency for businesses that serve the common good. The student may devote herself to the study of history or biology out of delight for the world God has made and the desire to investigate his work in it.

Yet the particular work of God in this time does not merely point us toward walking the way of Christ in any vocation or life situation we naturally find ourselves. Rather, it implies that, because of our special focus on joining God in his mission of building his kingdom through his church, we must constantly be asking how God might be calling us either to faithfulness to him in our present circumstances or to take up our cross and follow him out of those circumstances in service to him.

The unique characterization of this age—as one in which the culture of the kingdom of Christ is built by our proclamation of who he is and what he has done—means that our cultural priorities will probably look different from those non-Christians around us. We may give up a well-paying job to become a missionary in a far-off place. We may risk embarrassment and social stigmatization by asking our neighbors or coworkers if we can tell them about Jesus. Regardless, the reality of what Christ has done should radically reorganize how we live, what we do, and what we treasure.

This time between the times is certainly strange. We inhabit a period of history in which the most important clue to God's work in history has already happened and his great redemptive work is done. Yet it is never a static time, meant to be lived standing still. We anticipate his future return and remember his calling he left us with to proclaim the good news of Christ, and we step out into the way of Christ filled with the Spirit he has given us to form us into his image from now until the great resurrection in which we will be raised to life everlasting with him.

So how should we walk this way in the here and now? We have located the most important landmark on the map, but in order to triangulate our position and then navigate toward this goal, we still need some more landmarks.

Interpretation: Where Are We?

The first question of triangulation we have explored at length, and it is the one from which all others proceed. *When are we?* Knowing when we are in God's story of history helps us find our fixed bearing, our proper point of orientation: Christ in his incarnate life, death, and resurrection. The next question we need to ask is "Where are we?" In other words, what surrounds us? Where in the world are we, and in what cultural context do we each find ourselves at this moment?

We inhabit a particular time and place in which cultures shape everything about life. If we seek to answer how we should walk the way of Christ for our own time and place, we need to stop and look at what the specific cultural forms around us are saying about who we are, how to live, and the meaning of it all. This means that the second question is as much about exegesis as the first question. When we ask the orientation question of "When are we?" we seek to interpret what God has said to us in the Scriptures about the way things are and the way things ought to be. When we then turn to ask the interpretation question of "Where are we?" we look up from our Bibles to hear what our surrounding cultures are likewise saying about the way things are and ought to be.

Recall that as we discussed what culture is, we argued that culture consists of patterns of meaning by which we receive and construct an image of the world that we use to make sense of life. This means that culture is always speaking something, and God designed it this way. As we argued, the cultural mandate of Gen 1:27–28 connects culture with being God's imagers, and this implies that in our ways and products of culture we are always imaging something—or Someone. We are always offering an ordering to life that points toward God and the meaning that he has given to the world, or we are pointing away from it.

Some of the ways the cultures around us speak are obvious. When singers pen songs celebrating their abortions as expressions of liberation and justice, it is pretty clear that these are not words that Christians should sing along with. However, many ways that cultures speak are less obvious and require close examination for us to hear properly what they are saying. We must interpret culture and then make a judgment call on whether particular cultural forms help us or hinder us as we walk with Christ on the way. To help us in this, let us consider two different sets of questions that can help us interpret where we are and what is around us in our own times and places.

Worldview Question: What Is True?

Whether we realize it or not, we all live with a set of basic assumptions about the world. As Bavinck says, we all ask the following foundational questions: "What am I? What is the world, and what is my place and task within this world?"[4] How we each answer these questions provides us with a worldview. That is, a view of things from our own perspective that serves to integrate our perceptions about the world around us and make sense of them within a particular conceptual framework.[5] Our worldview functions to help us each answer the question "What is true?"

There are myriad resources on worldview, especially from a Christian perspective. Some offer inventories of religious commitments of various worldviews. Others seek to evaluate particular worldviews in relation to Christian convictions. Our interest here is not to offer a comprehensive description of worldview commitments or even to argue for the merit of a normative

---

[4] Herman Bavinck, *Christian Worldview*, trans. Nathaniel Gray Sutanto, James Eglinton, and Cory C. Brock (Wheaton, IL: Crossway, 2019), 4, 16.

[5] Nathaniel Gray Sutanto, James Eglinton, and Cory C. Brock describe this threefold function of a worldview in similarly cartographic terms as we have used here. They explain, "A worldview is a map, drawn over time from careful research, derived from actual knowledge of the geography, from pious religion, from the desire for truth, and it is amenable to updating. After all, maps are made from research—some careful, meticulous, and true and some not. Some maps account for the details as they are presented, and some are false. But map making we must do." Nathaniel Gray Sutanto, James Eglinton, and Cory C. Brock, "Editor's Introduction," in Bavinck, *Christian Worldview*, 7.

Christian worldview.[6] Rather, what we would like to point out as we explore the idea of worldview is that human beings are more than thinking minds, and the beliefs we hold about the world seem to be often settled intuitively more by what we have picked up from those around us than by the reasonableness of the ideas we come to embrace. As Jonathan Haidt argues, our motivations for believing certain things are often upstream from propositions about the world.[7]

Therefore, when someone provides an account of what is true within a particular cultural context, such an account is usually less about what that person has been *taught* about the world, so to speak, and more about what is *caught* from the way one's culture makes sense of the world and communicates that to one another through cultural forms. Charles Taylor calls this an intuited sense of the meaning of the world around us and the significance for how to we ought to live a "social imaginary."[8] That is, a social imaginary consists of the set of conditions about the world that whole societies have come to embrace as believable. As Taylor argues in *A Secular Age,* medieval Europe found unbelief in God as completely unbelievable—that is, not that atheism was impossible but rather that from their point of view a person simply could not live as if there were no God. They could not imagine a world in which belief in spiritual realities

---

[6] For a helpful evaluation of worldview thinking and a proposal in line with what we are offering here, see James Eglinton, "Editor's Introduction," in J. H. Bavinck, *Personality and Worldview*, trans. and ed. James Eglinton (Wheaton, IL: Crossway, 2023), 1–21.

[7] See Jonathan Haidt, *The Righteous Mind: Why Good People Are Divided by Politics and Religion* (New York: Vintage, 2013), esp. pt. 1.

[8] Charles Taylor, *A Secular Age* (Cambridge, MA: Belknap, 2007), 146, 171–72.

could be rejected. Today that has flipped: many in our society find belief in God and a transcendent reality to be unbelievable.[9]

As another example, many segments of our Western society today have come to embrace as completely unbelievable the idea that biological sex is a stable binary which in turn settles our identities as either male or female. In fact, many today find such an idea to be downright oppressive. The story of how we got to this point is complex.[10] What is simple enough to see, however, is that every inch of culture has become a battleground on this issue, ensuring that society is remade to coalesce with the mores of this social imaginary, even as the social imaginary is formed by culture. Check-in forms at the doctor's office, children's toy sections at the store, razor blades and makeup, and rainbow decals on sports teams' jerseys all flow out of and yet serve to prop up this social imaginary.

The point in all this is that culture and cultural products and worldviews are inextricably linked. Recall that culture, as we have described it, is the extension of human minds and human wills interacting with God's creation. When culture is formed or passed on, it is always imprinted in some way by the worldviews of cultural creators. To use the language of Christopher Watkin, culture is the way that we *figure* the world; and as such, when we encounter and receive culture, we receive something of the way others have figured the world.[11] When we participate

---

[9] See Taylor, 172–76.

[10] For a telling of this story, see Carl R. Trueman, *The Rise and Triumph of the Modern Self: Cultural Amnesia, Expressive Individualism, and the Road to the Sexual Revolution* (Wheaton, IL: Crossway, 2020).

[11] Christopher Watkin, *Biblical Critical Theory: How the Bible's Unfolding Story Makes Sense of Modern Life and Culture* (Grand Rapids: Zondervan Academic, 2022), 4–14.

with cultural forms or create them ourselves, we offer to others something of our worldview.

To answer the question, "Where are we?" we need to understand what is on offer through the cultures around us. That is, to begin to understand how we should walk the way of Christ in our own particular *cultural* time and place, we need to develop the skills to investigate the worldviews communicated in the cultural forms we encounter every day. Bavinck's three questions that worldviews function to answer, then, are a good place to start: What am I? What is the world? What is my place and task in the world?[12]

Let us consider an example of how we might examine a cultural object in light of these questions. Think about that little plastic card in your wallet. Though very useful in transactions at the store, they can speak very powerfully out of a particular worldview propped up by the banking system, marketing and brand managers, and a whole industry dedicated to retailing goods and services. What might credit cards say about *what I am?* If we listen closely to many of the messages used to recruit people to open accounts and use them prodigiously, we might hear that I am a purchaser, someone who exists to spend money. The world, in turn, is simply a reality oriented toward economic exchange, and my place in it is to buy things to meet my needs and make me happy.

Obviously, those are answers quite at odds with the way Scripture presents the world and its meaning. But does that mean responsible Christian cultural engagement requires abstaining completely from cultural forms like credit cards or retail shopping? Not necessarily. Understanding where we are on the map not only requires us to perceive the answers to worldview

---

[12] See Bavinck, *Christian Worldview*, 16.

questions that cultural forms communicate, but it also requires some further questions to guide how we ought to respond.

Worship Question: What Is Good and Desirable?

For many elements of culture that we encounter in our daily lives, the worldviews that have shaped those things, like credit cards, are often quite complex and less on the nose, so to speak. It is not clear whether they are serving to develop in us a worldview informed by Christian belief or by something else. In some cases, it can go either way.

The Wisdom literature of the Bible often refrains from painting life in black and white strokes. Much of what we encounter in life falls within the various tones of gray, neither clearly right or wrong, true or false. The book of Ecclesiastes instructs us that sometimes truly good things can be futile and vain (Eccl 1:1–11). Ecclesiastes and Proverbs also remind us that in some situations it is appropriate for us to do or celebrate something, while it could be that in those exact same situations it may be appropriate for us not to do that thing or even rebuke it (Eccl 3:1–8; Prov 26:4–5). The choices of following the wise way of Christ are often complex and not cast in tones of black and white. Even if we know the worldview giving shape to a particular cultural form, we need to ask some further questions to perceive what is truly good or desirable. Augustine reminds that it is often not the moral rightness or wrongness of a thing that we need to pay attention to, but rather its use.[13] Put simply,

---

[13] Augustine, *Teaching Christianity* (*De Doctrina Christiana*), trans. Edmund Hill (New York: New City, 1995), bk. 1, chs. 3, 4.

can this thing, like a credit card, be used to help me worship God? Does it help me bear the type of fruit in my life that is characteristic of life in Christ's kingdom?

No cultural form is neutral. As Dutch theologian J. H. Bavinck wrote, "Culture is religion made visible; it is religion actualized in the innumerable relations of daily life."[14] Because culture emerges from the minds and hearts of imagers, we either image God truly or falsely through culture, and so we are formed by culture to worship either him or something else.

We might encounter books about knowing Christ and devotion to him, and we might encounter books of spells and the celebration of the demonic. Both very clearly proceed from and are oriented to the worship of God or of something or someone else. But much of the culture we encounter is not always as clear in what it leads us to worship. For example, besides books about Jesus or Baphomet, we also find books about cooking, history, or children's literature. In these cases, such cultural forms might legitimately be directed toward the worship of God or away from him, depending on who is reading them, the context in which they emerge, and even the ideas they put forward. The task of cultural orientation involves our inquiring how each element of culture we interact with portrays what is truly good, desirable, and worth worshipping.

But we must not stop there. Christians, as cultural creators and shapers walking in the way of Christ, can even impart new meaning to existing culture. We can reuse and redirect culture in new ways, as Paul does in Acts 17:22–31 when he points to a statue to an unknown god. In this passage Paul argues that the

---

[14] J. H. Bavinck, *The Impact of Christianity on the Non-Christian World* (Grand Rapids: Eerdmans, 1948), 57.

cultural artifact the Athenians had constructed "in ignorance" actually anticipated Paul's presence with them that very day, making the God they did not know known truly and personally to them (Acts 17:23). Jesus models something similar in his conversation with the Samaritan woman at the well in John 4. In his confrontation with her over her past, she raises the issue of where God ought to be worshipped, highlighting the tension that divided Samaritans and Jews over the true temple of God. Jesus redirects this contentious element of culture that divided the Samaritans from the Jews and uses it to introduce her to his true identity as Savior of the world: "You Samaritans worship what you do not know. We worship what we do know, because salvation is from the Jews. But an hour is coming, and is now here, when the true worshipers will worship the Father in Spirit and in truth" (John 4:22–23).

Christians throughout the world have been doing things in similar ways for thousands of years. Just as many martyrs before and after her did, the Christian noblewoman Perpetua in the third century used her imprisonment and death in the Roman arena to offer a vision of Christ rather than the spectacle the people of Carthage sought. In *The City of God*, Augustine drew upon the history and civic pride of Rome to argue why Christians had not actually led to its downfall but had instead made it into a true city. The eighth-century monk Boniface famously cut down the sacred tree in central Germany dedicated to the worship of Thor, and then used its wood to build a church. More recently, Christians have used sports to disciple people in their faith, played board games to gather friends and neighbors around a table, and even employed artificial intelligence in service of Bible translation projects into languages that have never had the Bible before. The opportunities for redirecting culture unto the worship of God and obedience to his ways are endless.

This is because culture itself, as a patterning of creation with meaning and purpose, shapes and forms us at the very core of our existence. As James K. A. Smith argues, we encounter culture as public liturgies that direct our affections and teach us how to worship.[15] Culture communicates to us what we ought to behold as good and desirable, and so we must stop and reflect on exactly how various forms of culture we encounter form us and *what* they teach us to worship. If it is not God and his ways, then we have the opportunity to carefully and creatively redirect cultural forms toward that end.

Conclusion

TRIANGULATION: LOCATING OURSELVES ON THE MAP OF CULTURAL ENGAGEMENT

Orientation	When Are We?	What time is it?
		How should we live in the time in between?
Interpretation	Where Are We?	Worldview: What is true?
		Worship: What is good and desirable?

---

[15] James K. A. Smith, *Desiring the Kingdom: Worship, Worldview, and Cultural Formation*, in *Cultural Liturgies*, vol. 1 (Grand Rapids: Baker Academic, 2009).

To know where we are in God's story of history and thus to make sense of our own cultural moment in relation to the clues to history he has given, we need to orient ourselves to God's historical self-revelation in Christ and examine the world around us in light of God. This gives us the first two steps of our triangulation: (1) orientation toward the stable God-given landmarks of history and (2) interpretation of where our own time and place are in its convictions of worldview and worship. In the next chapter we turn to consider the final set of questions: Once we know when and where we are, how do we get to our final destination? How do we walk the way of Christ in this particular cultural moment in light of what Christ has revealed?

7

The Questions We Ask: Part 2

Pay careful attention, then, to how you
walk—not as unwise people but as wise.
—Ephesians 5:15

I n the previous chapter we began to explore the questions
we must ask to determine how we ought to engage culture
in our own particular time and place. Using the metaphor of
triangulating our position on a map, the first step is to get our
bearings by orienting to *when* we are in the story of history that
God is telling. That requires us to know the biblical story, which
is itself God's own forthtelling of universal history, so that we
can make sense of our own cultural moment in history in relation to him.

Next, we need to ask *where* we are in the great cultural
landscape of the world. This involves considering how the
culture we encounter offers to us something of the worldview

and worship of those who have shaped such cultural forms. As Christians being made into the image of Christ, we have the opportunity not only to perceive what such culture is communicating but also to redirect it and infuse it with new meaning, oriented toward Christ the Son of God.

Both of these sets of questions allow us to triangulate our own particular moment in history, the time and place in which we each live. Using our cartographic metaphor, one step still remains. Recall that our destination is the kingdom of Jesus Christ. Once we know where we are and where we seek to go on the map, we need to develop a strategy for how to get there.

Procession: How Do We Get There?

Traveling from one's current location to another destination on a map may look pretty easy. It can appear like a straight line—as the crow flies, as they say. But for anyone who has come up over a ridge only to see a lush valley of impenetrable rhododendron spread out before them, getting to a point far off on the horizon is a hard task. Those who are wise end up following creeks or stumbling upon a game trail or an established path that is already worn clear through the underbrush. The best way to traverse a wilderness is to consider how someone who has gone before has done it, evaluate if they have done it well, and if so, then follow their path.

Similarly, our final set of questions has to do with how we proceed on our way. How do we live here and now, in the midst of culture, knowing when and where we are, in order to rightly walk Christ's way and arrive at his kingdom fully come on earth?

To answer this, we need to consider *how* we should proceed and whether there are any examples we might follow.

How Should We Walk?

We have argued that Scripture presents us with a choice: to walk the way of Christ and advance his kingdom or to go the way of folly. Walking either way is always cultural, for the way is manifest *through* culture, and as we walk, culture *results*. What does this mean for our everyday lives? How should each of us walk here and now as we consider such things as our family, jobs, education, hobbies, and money? What about our votes, the type of food we cook, the music we hum along to, the novels we read, and the games we play? As we have said all along, in our model for cultural engagement we offer more questions than answers. This is because the complexities of culture present us with many things we might consider as we try to walk the way of Christ in culture.

Consider something as seemingly simple as a bicycle—which is something at least one of us authors considers to be a truly magnificent product of culture. We can pursue cultural excellence in giving special attention to the form and function of a bicycle so that we can ride fast—relatively speaking—up and down mountains, through hairpin turns, and across city blocks. We can also pursue the simple delight of teaching a child how to ride a bike that we bought for next to nothing at the local thrift store. It seems that a bicycle is a product of culture truly worth celebrating and enjoying.

But even if the idea of a bicycle is something that fills us with awe and wonder, the reality of a particular bicycle can be quite complex. How much is wise to pay for a bicycle? Who made the bicycle, and should I support the industry that they labor in? Was this bicycle now in my possession stolen? Even more questions arise as we think about how we should ride a bicycle. You can ride a bike across rural China laden with Bibles to give to persecuted house churches. You can ride a bike to the store to buy food for your family. Many people throughout the world do so every day. But you can also ride a bike with the local gang of middle schoolers recruited to deliver drugs for a dealer. You can ride a bike in a race to triumph in a sport that you have so devoted yourself to that you cheat and lie and put others down to advance your own career.

How might we answer the questions of walking the way of Christ and advancing his kingdom through the culture of a bicycle? Perhaps only by asking further questions: What is my aim in riding this bike? Is it a worthy goal that can be directed toward the worship of Christ and love of neighbor? Are there ways that I can ride this bike well, and are there ways that I can ride it poorly? Such questions may seem pedantic, but if we remember that every cultural endeavor presents us with a choice either to walk in the way of Christ or not, every time we put a foot on the pedal to set off should give us pause. We would do well to consider where we are going and how we should get there.

To put it more simply, such questions ultimately come down to two that we should always be asking: How do I walk the way of Christ in this particular situation? How do I advance the ways of the King and his kingdom with this specific cultural form? We each might legitimately answer these questions differently depending on our context. This certainly does not imply some great relative principle in which everyone should be like Israel and do what is right in our own eyes (Judg 17:6). We have both God's inspired Word and the guidance of the Holy Spirit to direct us. But that is not all. We also have the wisdom of those who have gone before us to draw upon. Faithful Christians from other times and places can offer inspiration for us to consider as we triangulate when and where we are and how to walk—especially if they encountered cultural circumstances similar to those we encounter. Thus, our last question looks at whom we can follow as we set out on our way.

Whom Can We Follow?

Hebrews 11 reminds us that the faithful who have gone before us had faith in God's promises. The author of Hebrews then implores us in 12:1 that this great cloud of witnesses should inspire us in our own faith and in the pursuit of the way of Christ. Indeed, the example of faithful Christians who model wise cultural engagement in their own times and places can help us know how to approach the challenges of cultural engagement we encounter in our own context. When we think about whose example we could follow, we find no shortage of worthy models. We could consider the Garo Christians of Bangladesh, who penned the famous hymn "I Have Decided to Follow Jesus" when thousands converted to Christ amid a hostile Islamic culture.[1] Likewise, we could consider the many Christians who

---

[1] Michael Hawn, "History of Hymns: 'I Have Decided to Follow Jesus,'" Discipleship Ministries, June 10, 2020, https://www.umcdiscipleship.org/articles/history-of-hymns-i-have-decided-to-follow-jesus.

fought for the abolition of slavery throughout the Western world, such as William Wilberforce, Frederick Douglass, and Sojourner Truth. Or we could take inspiration from the countless Christian plumbers, nurses, English teachers, and nannies who have all engaged culture wisely in the unseen and unsung tasks of everyday life.

There would no doubt be great benefit in considering each of those examples. However, what we offer now are glimpses of several individuals located within a particular faith tradition that seems especially fruitful for thinking about culture today. Both of us authors have been shaped by the theology of culture offered by the Dutch neo-Calvinist tradition, and we have drawn upon its thinkers like Abraham Kuyper and Herman Bavinck frequently throughout this book. In many ways, this is not surprising. What distinguishes neo-Calvinism, as Cory Brock and Gray Sutanto argue, is the way it retrieves classical Reformed theology when many others in the nineteenth-century Dutch context departed from orthodoxy, and yet neo-Calvinism spoke in and to conversations and categories of modern philosophy and theology.[2] This theological movement is not only concerned with issues of cultural engagement but is itself an example of a robust theological enculturation of the Christian faith to meet the worldview and worship challenges of its own time and place.

Therefore, we conclude this chapter with a look at four different figures informed by the Dutch neo-Calvinist tradition.[3]

---

[2] Cory C. Brock and N. Gray Sutanto, *Neo-Calvinism: A Theological Introduction* (Bellingham: Lexham Academic, 2022), 4.

[3] The fathers of Dutch neo-Calvinism, Abraham Kuyper and Herman Bavinck, could be considered worthy models for cultural

As we think about their unique contributions, we frame them as working out several core convictions of a neo-Calvinist theology of culture for a particular time and place. Each adheres to the conviction that God is in control of history, that culture is deeply related to God's purpose for humanity, and that Christians ought to relate their faith to every element of culture they encounter. Their differences are ones of tone and tenor, due in part to the particular way they articulate the Christian's response to culture in a given time and place, complete with the callings and urgencies presented by that context.[4]

---

engagement. However, we have aimed to present here figures in the tradition who are closer to our own time and place. Though they witnessed the First World War at the end of their lives, neither Kuyper nor Bavinck lived to see the Second World War, and the great realism that marks postwar theologians who witnessed the global atrocities and the decline of Western imperialism is not prominent in their thought. The four figures we have chosen here each provide a neo-Calvinist approach to cultural engagement more in tune with the realities we face in the twenty-first century.

[4] This approach of highlighting how neo-Calvinism has been adapted to four different places and times takes inspiration from Aaron Renn's three-part typology of contemporary evangelicalism. Renn argues that there have been "three worlds of evangelicalism": the positive world of pre-1944, in which society was largely positive toward Christianity; the neutral world of 1994–2014, in which society was neither friendly nor openly hostile but simply tolerant; and the negative world of 2014 to today, in which Christianity is actively resisted by society at large. Aaron M. Renn, "The Three Worlds of Evangelicalism," *First Things*, February 1, 2022, https://www.firstthings.com/article/2022/02/the-three-worlds-of-evangelicalism.

Klaas Schilder: Cultural Engagement in War Zones

Writing and teaching a generation after Kuyper, Dutch theologian Klaas Schilder (1890–1952) developed a model for cultural engagement well adapted to the challenges faced by Dutch society in the mid-twentieth century. He witnessed both world wars, was imprisoned during the 1940s Nazi occupation of the Netherlands, and then spent the rest of the Second World War in hiding because of persecution. Such societal upheaval, combined with infighting in Schilder's denomination, solidified his priorities toward culture as ones of prophetic resistance and bold resilience. Schilder became a fighter fit for cultural wartime.[5]

Like Kuyper and Bavinck, Schilder understood culture as a gift from God. More than this, he understood culture as a calling, a task for God's people to fulfill as they lived out his designs for human beings.[6] As a calling, Schilder understood culture to be something humans can be faithful or unfaithful toward. He argued that culture always proceeds from one's religious convictions. Christians and non-Christians share the same cultural workshop, he said, but what they make with the tools God has given them are vastly different. While sinful humans, dead in their sins, craft idols, Christians made alive in the Spirit bring forth cultural treasures for the worship of Christ and the

---

[5] See "General Introduction," in Klaas Schilder, *The Klaas Schilder Reader: The Essential Theological Writings*, ed. George Harinck, Marinus de Jong, and Richard Mouw, trans. Albert Gootjes and Albert Oosterhoff (Bellingham: Lexham Academic, 2022), 1–19.

[6] See Klaas Schilder, *Christ and Culture*, ed. Jochem Douma, trans. William Helder and Albert H. Oosterhoff (Hamilton ON: Lucerna CRTS, 2016), 145–46.

expanse of his kingdom.[7] For this reason, Christians should pursue true cultural communion with fellow Christians and work to develop cultural forms and patterns of life that build the church and support God's mission in the world.

Schilder teaches us that in some times and places, the divide between Christians and non-Christians on issues of worldview or worship is so wide that faithfulness to God's cultural calling to walk in his ways means we resist cultural influences, remove ourselves from cultural settings, and redirect culture for the very survival of the church.[8] According to Schilder's example, how might we walk in Christ's way in trying times? By developing distinctly Christian patterns of life separate from the world. Many places in the world may need such dedication to preserving the Christian faith by living the Christian life with such focus and trepidation. There is a danger in this, though. Namely, lapsing into a perpetual alarmism that leads us always to fight the cultural influences around us even after the war's intensity has subsided.

Richard Mouw: Cultural Engagement in Places of Peace

While he certainly appreciates the counterbalance of Schilder, contemporary neo-Calvinist professor and theologian Richard Mouw (b. 1940) offers a theology of culture of a much more optimistic tone.[9] Mouw reminds us that God truly cares about

---

[7] See Schilder, *Christ and Culture*, 110, 174.

[8] Schilder, 137–38.

[9] See Mouw's own comments assessing his approach offered "in a spirit quite different from Schilder," in Richard J. Mouw, "Klaas

culture.[10] Culture is God's gift to humanity to image him and reveal his beauty, and it is preserved and even developed toward its original goal, despite the reality of sin, by God's common grace.[11] As we encounter culture, we have the opportunity to celebrate what is truly good in what we see and to worship God through it. Christians can and should collaborate with non-Christians in cultural creation when it serves the common good.[12]

This presents a compelling model of cultural engagement for peacetime. When Christians and non-Christians coexist within a robust societal valuing of pluralism—the idea that

---

Schilder as Public Theologian," *Covenant Theological Journal* 38 (2003): 285.

[10] Richard J. Mouw, *All that God Cares About: Common Grace and Divine Delights* (Grand Rapids: Brazos, 2020).

[11] In this study, we have intentionally not utilized the doctrine of common grace, which figures prominently in the thought of many of the neo-Calvinist theologians we have engaged with in this section. According to Abraham Kuyper, common grace is the belief that God both providentially withholds the full effects of humanity's sin and leads creation forward toward his goals for history, because he loves what he has made. See Kuyper, *Common Grace: God's Gifts for a Fallen World*, vol. 2, *The Doctrinal Sections*, ed. Jordan J. Ballor and J. Daryl Charles, trans. Nelson D. Kloosterman and Ed M. Van der Maas (Bellingham, WA: Lexham, 2019), 645. God provides special saving grace to the elect, but to all his creatures he gives a common grace which ensures they can exist and live in some way according to his original designs. While the doctrine of common grace is certainly helpful in the discussion of how culture is possible and, in light of this, in what way Christians should live, the debate over its validity and what exactly the doctrine entails is ongoing. We have set all of that aside for discussion of a later day.

[12] Mouw, *All That God Cares About*, 52.

various religious viewpoints should be tolerated because of a commitment to religious freedom—then Christians and non-Christians can work together in producing culture that blesses everyone. The beauty of art, a just economy, and community soccer leagues are all things that honor God because they help all of us be more human, according to his cultural designs for humanity living together.

For many Christians today, we need to hear that God actually cares about culture and that culture is not simply something to think about in terms of how to evangelize our neighbors or assess worldview issues we encounter. As Mouw argues, culture is something God created human beings for, and as such it has value on its own.[13] This realization may free many Christians to suddenly look up and see that there are truly beautiful and good things in the world that honor God, even if they were created by someone who does not know God in a saving way.

Mouw's model never ceases to be relevant, for we should all pursue an attitude of wonder and awe at God through his creation in the language that our hearts and minds speak: culture. Likewise, we should all aspire to live peaceably with our neighbors and to love our communities well through constructive and creative cultural engagement. However, if Schilder's model of wartime cultural engagement can lapse into pessimistic alarmism and Christian cultural isolation when the culture war is not hot, this model can be too optimistic for contexts in which society seems aligned against core Christian convictions.

---

[13] Mouw, 76–80.

Tim Keller: Cultural Engagement in Transitional Spaces

Contemporary pastor Tim Keller (1950–2023), who ministered for decades in New York City, offers an alternative model to both Schilder and Mouw, yet still from within the broadly neo-Calvinist theology of cultural engagement. Keller was known for his winsome apologetic of the Christian faith. He proposes a self-professed "third way" that aims to rise above the partisan culture wars in order to offer to a skeptical world a fresh glimpse of how Christianity constructs both a compelling and a truly inhabitable world.[14] For Keller, engagement with the ideas and patterns of meaning of cultures—specifically urban, post-Christian cultures—is essential for two missiologically oriented reasons. First, it is essential because it helps Christians witness by knowing what non-Christians are actually skeptical of concerning the faith. Second, it is essential because culture is always the medium by which the beauty of the Christian faith is embodied for a watching world. When the faith is lived out, it always is done within a cultural context and in relation in some way to that context's cultural forms.

Surprisingly, in recent years Keller faced no shortage of criticism from Christians themselves. This is due to the assertion that Keller represents an approach to cultural engagement out of touch with the actual cultural moment in which we live. Some have argued that Keller's winsome way may have been appropriate for when Western society was positive or even neutral toward Christianity, but today cultural moods

---

[14] Timothy Keller, *The Reason for God: Belief in an Age of Skepticism* (New York: Penguin, 2009), xxv–xxvi.

in the West are so hostile toward Christianity that what is needed is active resistance against secularism for the sake of Christian religious freedom, let alone Christian witness.[15] There may be some truth to this critique of Keller. Our world is rapidly changing, and increasingly Christians find themselves ridiculed within mainstream society and even susceptible to legal penalties for professing belief in things like sin and marriage. However, to say Keller provides a model for Christian cultural engagement in times when our faith is neutrally tolerated seems to miss what Keller has modeled for us.

Much of Keller's ministry has taken place in transitional spaces—cultural contexts in which tectonic worldview changes have been happening rapidly. Late modernity has witnessed not a reduction of spirituality, as some secularists predicted, but rather an explosion of alternative spiritualities.[16] Our age seems less concerned with questions of what is true and more concerned with what visions of the world are believable and inhabitable. Keller aims to provide a cultural apologetic for Christianity for just this sort of context. He models how Christians—in such times and places in which culture reveals radical transition in how people make sense of the world—can pay attention to the changing patterns of meaning communicated through culture. For Keller, Christians must find new ways to communicate the core truths of Christianity in and through cultural forms that resonate with the increasingly skeptical people around them.

---

[15] James R. Wood, "How I Evolved on Tim Keller," *First Things*, May 6, 2022, https://www.firstthings.com/web-exclusives/2022/05 /how-i-evolved-on-tim-keller.

[16] See, for example, Tara Isabella Burton, *Strange Rites: New Religions for a Godless World* (New York: Public Affairs, 2020).

Certainly, this can err in the direction of appeasement or compromising the faith to accommodate the moral or cultural sensibilities of those around us. We might get so eager to show how Christianity creates a cultural world that is respectable and appealing that we actually construct it in such an accommodating way that it appeals in wrong ways that are contrary to orthodox Christian convictions. But it seems this is not the inevitable result of Keller's approach, just a danger of it. We would do well to follow his example as we find ourselves in transitional spaces in which the vague memory of Christian truth that a society possesses has become an inaccurate caricature, with the result that non-Christians need Christians to culturally communicate the gospel in ways they might be able to receive it. How might we do this? By walking the way of Christ in our particular cultural time and place.

Johann Herman Bavinck: Cultural Engagement in Pioneering Places

Finally, if Keller provides a model for engaging culture in places that have a memory of former Christian influence upon culture, what about those places that have no such memory and need a pioneering encounter with Christ and his way? Dutch missiologist Johann Herman Bavinck (1895–1964) provides just such a framework for us. The nephew of the famous theologian Herman Bavinck, J. H. Bavinck spent many years as a missionary in Indonesia and in the last decades of his life was a professor in the Netherlands who wrote on theology, mission, and worldview. Importantly, J. H. Bavinck was particularly interested in the way various cultural contexts expressed the religious beliefs about the people who created such culture, as well as how religious beliefs themselves shape and drive the development of culture. For J. H. Bavinck, human beings are fundamentally religious by virtue of being creatures made in God's image, who are ordered toward worship of something that is ultimate and who are motivated by design to understand and order their world by such ultimate things.[17]

Therefore, for J. H. Bavinck, culture is not merely a window into understanding the central religious convictions of a people but is itself the mode in which any religious conviction about ultimate matters is lived out. This is an important observation in thinking about Christian cultural engagement because it offers a way of understanding culture as always full of connecting points between the vision of the world offered by Christian Scripture and the way individuals in non-Christian cultures view the world.

Specifically, J. H. Bavinck offers five "magnetic points" that arise out of the "universal religious consciousness" every human being has by nature, and these magnetic points are important for mission because they offer advice on how to speak in culturally appropriate ways to non-Christians about the truth of Scripture.[18] These points include, first, the conceptual relationship every person has of how they relate to the

---

[17] J. H. Bavinck, *The Church between Temple and Mosque: A Study of the Relationship between Christianity and Other Religions*, ed. Daniel Strange (Glenside, PA: Westminster Seminary Press, 2023), 9–17.

[18] Bavinck, *The Church between Temple and Mosque*, 24–28. For an accessible summary of these five points, see Daniel Strange, *Making Faith Magnetic: Five Hidden Themes Our Culture Can't Stop*

cosmos, the entire world around them. Second, everyone has a sense of norms of right and wrong that must be obeyed. Third, everyone wrestles with the meaning of our existence and what will be our future destiny. Fourth, everyone has a sense that things are not as they should be, and therefore there is a need for some sort of salvation. Fifth, and finally, everyone has a sense that a supreme power, that we are somehow related to, exists behind reality.[19]

As J. H. Bavinck would come to argue, how individuals construct beliefs about the world and their place in it, according to the categories of these five magnetic points, serves to construct what J. H. Bavinck calls a "worldvision," which shapes the common cultural patterns of life of a people.[20] The task of Christians engaging culture in pioneering contexts is to pay attention to the way a culture reveals what a people believes about the five magnetic points, and then to offer ways of thinking Christianly about those magnetic points in culturally informed ways. This is to find connections and common ground with those unfamiliar with or who otherwise reject the Christian faith.

But J. H. Bavinck's example for cultural engagement for us is not merely that we ought to think this way as we encounter cultures and religions quite different from our own. Rather, J. H. Bavinck wisely stresses for us that it matters what our attitude is when we do so.[21] To think like a missionary in a

---

Talking About . . . and How to Connect Them to Christ (Epsom, UK: The Good Book Company, 2021).

[19] Bavinck, *The Church between Temple and Mosque,* 26–28.

[20] James Eglinton, "Editor's Introduction" in J. H. Bavinck, *Personality and Worldview,* ed. and trans. James Eglinton (Wheaton, IL: Crossway, 2023), 12.

[21] Bavinck, *The Church between Temple and Mosque,* 189–190.

pioneering context, we must forgo any pretense that our culture is somehow superior and that non-Christians are somehow primitive and ignorant for inhabiting their culture informed by such unbiblical beliefs. We must rid ourselves of any pride that causes us to miss the fact that our own culture is not synonymous with the truth of Scripture. For though our own culture is often shaped by our belief in Christ, the way that Christ might shape the culture of someone else far removed from our context may result in Christian cultural expressions very different from our own. We must not shy away from witnessing to the way of Christ. Rather, as we do witness to the way of Christ, we should expect that others will walk in that way differently than we do as the gospel takes root in different times and places, shaping culture in new and beautiful ways.[22]

TRIANGULATION: LOCATING OURSELVES ON THE MAP OF CULTURAL ENGAGEMENT

Orientation	When Are We?	What time is it?
		How should we live in the time in between?
Interpretation	Where Are We?	Worldview: What is true?
		Worship: What is good and desirable?
Procession	How Do We Get There?	How should we walk?
		Whom can we follow?

---

[22] Bavinck, 193, 199.

CONCLUSION

How happy are those whose way is blameless, who
walk according to the LORD's instruction! Happy are
those who keep his decrees and seek him with all their
heart. They do nothing wrong; they walk in his ways.
—Psalm 119:1–3

So, whether you eat or drink, or whatever you
do, do everything for the glory of God.
—1 Corinthians 10:31

In this book we have offered a framework for how Christians
should think about culture. We have argued that the Bible
from start to finish tells a unified story of God's work in his
world and that human culture is a key part of this. Throughout
the book we have made it clear that culture itself is not the ultimate goal of the story, even if it is ever-present in the narrative.
As God's creatures made to image him, we are called to walk
in the way of Christ who is the great image of God, *par excellence*. This way of Christ is always a cultural path lived out in
particular times and places, and cultural forms and products are

the inevitable result of people traveling this path. Moreover, following Christ in his way requires that we pay attention to where we are in history and to what cultural context surrounds us, and then to consider the example of others as we set off on this way in our own time and place.

This basic framework for cultural engagement can serve students, pastors, mothers, plumbers, lawyers, athletes, truck drivers, and songwriters as they seek to walk with Christ in their vocations, homes, hobbies, and civic responsibilities—indeed their entire cultural life. Moreover, this framework can offer a way for Christians to inhabit their cultural context, with all of their vocations, responsibilities, and callings in view, all the more urgently as Christians with a particular calling to proclaim the King and advance the ways of his kingdom until he comes again.

If you take away nothing else from this book, let it be this: Christ Jesus tells us that he himself is "the way, the truth, and the life" (John 14:6). If we are called to follow his example and walk his wise way in all our *culturing*—in all our cooking, commuting, tweeting, sleeping, visiting the sick, and voting in elections—then we must keep Christ, with his words and actions, ever before us. Surely the Christian life is nothing less than beholding our Lord Jesus as the great goal of all time and place. We aim to behold him, and by seeing him, we are drawn ever toward the vision of the living God, walking in his ways until we are made complete and mature in his image (2 Cor 3:18). "Blessed are the pure in heart, for they will see God" (Matt 5:8).

And this is the greatest *cultural* calling.

SELECTED BIBLIOGRAPHY

The Ante-Nicene Fathers. Edited by Alexander Roberts, James Donaldson, Philip Schaff, and Henry Wace. 10 vols. Peabody, MA: Hendrickson, 1996.

Aristotle. *Nicomachean Ethics.* 3rd ed. Translated by Terence Irwin. Indianapolis: Hackett, 2019.

Ashford, Bruce Riley. *Every Square Inch: An Introduction to Cultural Engagement for Christians.* Bellingham, WA: Lexham, 2015.

————, and Craig G. Bartholomew. *The Doctrine of Creation: A Constructive Kuyperian Approach.* Downers Grove, IL: IVP Academic, 2020.

Auerbach, Erich. *Mimesis: The Representation of Reality in Western Literature.* Princeton, NJ: Princeton University, 2003.

Augustine. *The City of God.* Edited by Boniface Ramsey. Translated by William Babcok. New York: New City, 2013.

————. *Teaching Christianity.* Translated by Edmund Hill. New York: New City, 1995.

————. *The Trinity.* 2nd ed. Edited by Edmund Hill and John E. Rotelle. New York: New City, 2012.

Bacote, Vincent. *The Political Disciple: A Theology of Public Life.* Grand Rapids: Zondervan, 2015.

―――. *The Spirit in Public Theology: Appropriating the Legacy of Abraham Kuyper.* Eugene, OR: Wipf and Stock, 2010.

Bailey, Justin Ariel. *Interpreting Your World: Five Lenses for Engaging Theology and Culture.* Grand Rapids: Baker Academic, 2022.

Bartholomew, Craig G., and Ryan P. O'Dowd. *Old Testament Wisdom Literature: A Theological Introduction.* Downers Grove, IL: IVP Academic, 2011.

Bavinck, Herman. *Christian Worldview.* Translated by Nathaniel Gray Sutanto, James Eglinton, and Cory C. Brock. Wheaton, IL: Crossway, 2019.

―――. *Philosophy of Revelation: A New Annotated Edition.* Edited by Nathaniel Gray Sutanto and Cory Brock. Peabody, MA: Hendrickson, 2018.

―――. *Reformed Dogmatics: Abridged in One Volume.* Edited by John Bolt. Grand Rapids: Baker Academic, 2011.

―――. *Reformed Dogmatics: Volume 2: God and Creation.* Edited by John Bolt. Translated by John Vriend. Grand Rapids: Baker Academic, 2004.

―――. *Reformed Dogmatics: Volume 3: Sin and Salvation in Christ.* Edited by John Bolt. Translated by John Vriend. Grand Rapids: Baker Academic, 2006.

Bavinck, Johann Herman. *The Church between Temple and Mosque: A Study of the Relationship between Christianity and Other Religions.* Edited by Daniel Strange. Glenside, PA: Westminster Seminary, 2023.

―――. *The Impact of Christianity on the Non-Christian World.* Grand Rapids: Eerdmans, 1948.

————. *Personality and Worldview.* Translated and edited by James Eglinton. Wheaton, IL: Crossway, 2023.

Bettenson, Henry, and Chris Maunder. *Documents of the Christian Church.* 4th Edition. Oxford: Oxford University, 2011.

Bird, Michael F., and Scott Harrower, eds. *Trinity Without Hierarchy: Reclaiming Nicene Orthodoxy in Evangelical Theology.* Grand Rapids: Kregel Academic, 2019.

Blocher, Henri. "The Fear of the Lord as the 'Principle' of Wisdom." *Tyndale Bulletin* 28 (1977): 27.

————. *In the Beginning: The Opening Chapters of Genesis.* Downers Grove, IL: IVP, 1984.

Brock, Cory C., and N. Gray Sutanto. *Neo-Calvinism: A Theological Introduction.* Bellingham, WA: Lexham Academic, 2022.

Brooks, David. *The Road to Character.* New York: Random House Trade, 2016.

Burton, Tara Isabella. *Strange Rites: New Religions for a Godless World.* New York: Public Affairs, 2020.

Carson, D.A. *Christ and Culture Revisited.* Grand Rapids: Eerdmans, 2008.

Carter, Craig A. *Rethinking Christ and Culture: A Post-Christendom Perspective.* Grand Rapids: Brazos, 2006.

Charles, J. Daryl. *Our Secular Vocation: Rethinking the Church's Calling to the Marketplace.* Brentwood, TN: B&H Academic, 2023.

D'Andrade, Roy. "Some Kinds of Casual Power That Make Up Culture." In *Explaining Culture Scientifically.* Edited by Melissa J. Brown, 19–36. Seattle: University of Washington Press, 2008.

Davingon, Phil. *Practicing Christians, Practical Atheists: How Cultural Liturgies and Everyday Social Practices Shape the Christian Life*. Eugene, OR: Cascade, 2023.

Dumbrell, William, J. *Creation and Covenant: An Old Testament Covenant Theology*. Milton Keynes, UK: Paternoster, 2013.

Dyrness, William. *The Facts on the Ground: A Wisdom Theology of Culture*. Eugene, OR: Cascade, 2021.

Edgar, William. *Created and Creating: A Biblical Theology of Culture*. Downers Grove, IL: IVP Academic, 2016.

Goheen, Michael. *Introducing Christian Mission Today: Scripture, History, and Issues*. Downers Grove, IL: IVP Academic, 2014.

———— and Craig Bartholomew. *The True Story of the Whole World: Finding Your Place in the Biblical Drama*. Grand Rapids: Brazos, 2020.

Goudzwaard, Bob and Craig Bartholomew. *Beyond the Modern Age: An Archaeology of Contemporary Culture*. Downers Grove, IL: IVP Academic, 2017.

Grant, Robert. *Irenaeus of Lyons*. Nashville: Routledge, 1997.

Haidt, Johnathan. *The Righteous Mind: Why Good People Are Divided by Politics and Religion*. New York: Vintage, 2013.

Hollinger, P. Dennis. *Head, Heart and Hands: Bringing Together Christian Thought, Passion and Action*. Downers Grove, IL: IVP, 2005.

Keller, Timothy. *Center Church: Doing Balanced, Gospel-Centered Ministry in Your City*. Grand Rapids: Zondervan, 2012.

————. *The Reason for God: Belief in an Age of Skepticism*. New York: Penguin, 2009.

Kuyper, Abraham. *Abraham Kuyper: A Centennial Reader.* Edited by James D. Bratt. Grand Rapids: Eerdmans, 1998.

———. *Common Grace: God's Gifts for a Fallen World: Volume 2: The Doctrinal Section.* Edited by Jordan J. Ballor and J. Daryl Charles. Translated by Nelson D. Kloosterman and Ed M. Van der Maas. Collected Works in Public Theology. Bellingham, WA: Lexham, 2019.

Long, Stephen D. *Theology and Culture: A Guide to the Discussion.* Eugene, OR: Cascade, 2008.

MacIntyre, Alasdair. *After Virtue: A Study in Moral Theory.* 3rd Edition. Notre Dame, IN: University of Notre Dame, 2007.

Moreau, A. Scott. *Contextualization in World Missions: Mapping and Assessing Evangelical Models.* Grand Rapids: Kregel, 2012.

Mouw, Richard J. *All that God Cares About: Common Grace and Divine Delights.* Grand Rapids: Brazos, 2020.

———. "Klaas Schilder as Public Theologian." *CTJ* 38 (2003): 285.

Newbigin, Lesslie. *Foolishness to the Greeks: The Gospel and Western Culture.* Grand Rapids: Eerdmans, 1988.

———. *The Gospel in a Pluralist Society.* Grand Rapids: Eerdmans, 1989.

———. *The Household of God: Lectures on the Nature of the Church.* Eugene, OR: Wipf and Stock, 2008.

The Nicene and Post-Nicene Fathers. Edited by Alexander Roberts, James Donaldson, Philip Shaff, and Henry Wace. 14 vols. Peabody, MA: Hendrickson, 1995.

Niebuhr, Richard. *Christ and Culture.* 50th Anniversary Expanded Edition. San Francisco: Harper & Row, 2001.

O'Donovan, Oliver. *Begotten or Made?* Tryon, SC: Davenant, 2022.

———. *Resurrection and Moral Order: An Outline for Evangelical Ethics.* 2nd Edition. Grand Rapids: Eerdmans, 1994.

Peterson, Eugene. *Christ Plays in Ten Thousand Places: A Conversation in Spiritual Theology.* Grand Rapids: Eerdmans, 2005.

———. *The Jesus Way: A Conversation on the Ways That Jesus Is the Way.* Grand Rapids: Eerdmans, 2007.

Plantinga, Cornelius. *Engaging God's World: A Christian Vision of Faith, Learning, and Living.* Grand Rapids: Eerdmans, 2002.

Plato. *Plato: Complete Works.* Edited by John M. Cooper and D. S. Hutchinson. Indianapolis: Hackett, 1997.

Quinn, Benjamin T. *Walking in God's Wisdom: The Book of Proverbs.* Bellingham, WA: Lexham, 2021.

———, and Walter R. Strickland II. *Every Waking Hour: An Introduction to Work and Vocation for Christians.* Bellingham, WA: Lexham, 2016.

Reeve, William. *The Apology of Tertullian.* N.p.: Creative Media Partners, 2018.

Renn, Aaron M., "The Three Worlds of Evangelicalism," *First Things* (1 February 2022) https://www.firstthings.com/article/2022/02/the-three-worlds-of-evangelicalism.

Schilder, Klaas. *Christ and Culture.* Edited by Jochem Douma. Translated by William Helder and Albert H. Oosterhoff. Hamilton, ON: Lucerna CRTS, 2016.

———. *The Klaas Schilder Reader: The Essential Theological Writings.* Edited by George Harinck, Marinus de Jong, and Richard Mouw. Translated by Albert Gootjes and Albert Oosterhoff. Bellingham, WA: Lexham Academic, 2022.

Smith, James K.A. *Desiring the Kingdom: Worship, Worldview, and Cultural Formation*. Vol. 1 of *Cultural Liturgies*. Grand Rapids: Baker Academic, 2009.

———. *How to Inhabit Time: Understanding the Past, Facing the Future, Living Faithfully Now*. Grand Rapids: Brazos, 2022.

———. *On the Road with Saint Augustine: A Real-World Spirituality for Restless Hearts*. Grand Rapids: Brazos, 2019.

———. *You Are What You Love*. Grand Rapids: Baker Academic, 2016.

Spykman, Gordon. *Reformational Theology: A New Paradigm for Doing Dogmatics*. Grand Rapids: Eerdmans, 1992.

Strange, Daniel. *Making Faith Magnetic: Five Hidden Themes Our Culture Can't Stop Talking About . . . and How to Connect Them to Christ*. Epsom, UK: The Good Book Company, 2011.

———. *Plugged In: Connecting Your Faith With What You Watch, Read, and Play*. Epsom, UK: The Good Book Company, 2019.

Taylor, Charles. *A Secular Age*. Cambridge, MA: Belknap, 2007.

Troeltsch, Ernst. *The Social Teaching of the Christian Churches*. Translated by Olive Wyon. 2 vols. New York: MacMillan, 1931.

Trueman, Carl R. *The Rise and Triumph of the Modern Self: Cultural Amnesia, Expressive Individualism, and the Road to Sexual Revolution*. Wheaton, IL: Crossway, 2020.

Vanhoozer, Kevin J. "What is Everyday Theology? How and Why Christians Should Read Culture." In *Everyday Theology: How to Read Cultural Texts and Interpret Trends*, edited by Kevin J. Vanhoozer, Charles A. Anderson, and Michael J. Sleasman, 15-62. Grand Rapids: Baker Academic, 2007.

Van Leeuwen, Raymond. *Dictionary for Theological Interpretation of the Bible.* Edited by Kevin J. Vanhoozer. Grand Rapids: Baker Academic, 2005.

———. "Book of Proverbs." In *DTIB*, 638–641.

———. "Proverbs." In *Introduction to Wisdom Literature: The Book of Proverbs, the Book of Ecclesiastes, the Song of Songs, the Book of Wisdom, the Book of Sirach*, edited by Leander E. Keck and Richard J. Clifford. *New Interpreter's Bible: A Commentary in Twelve Volumes* 5. Nashville: Abingdon, 1997.

———. "Liminality and Worldview in Proverbs 1–9." *Semeia* 50 (1990): 111–44.

Veenhof, Jan. *Nature and Grace in Herman Bavinck.* Translated by Albert M. Wolters. Sioux Center, IA: Dordt College, 2006.

Watkin, Christopher. *Biblical Critical Theory: How the Bible's Unfolding Story Makes Sense of Modern Life and Culture.* Grand Rapids: Zondervan Academic, 2022.

Willard, Dallas. *Renovation of the Heart: Putting on the Character of Christ.* 20th anniversary ed. Colorado Springs: NavPress, 2021.

Williams, Raymond. *Keywords: A Vocabulary of Culture and Society.* Rev. ed. New York: Oxford University, 1976.

Wolters, Al. *Creation Regained: Biblical Basics for a Reformational Worldview.* 2nd Edition. Grand Rapids: Eerdmans, 2005.

SUBJECT INDEX

A

Abel, 11
abolition of slavery, 124
Abraham; Abram, 12, 14, 16,
    52, 63–64
activism; activist, 35, 41
Adam, 8–9, 11, 23, 60, 104
Adorno, Theodor, 35
Alighieri, Dante. *See* Dante
Anabaptist movement;
    Anabaptists, 41, 43–44,
    54, 57
Ananias, 66
Apostles' Creed, 61–62, 68
Aquinas, Thomas, 47, 50–51
artifacts (cultural), 28–29
atheism, 111
Athenians, 116
Auerbach, Erich, 34
Augustine, 21, 40, 49–51, 87,
    101–2, 114, 116

B

Babylonians, 15

Bangladesh, 123
Baphomet, 115
baptism, 43, 66–67, 94
Bavinck, Herman, 51–58, 63,
    68–69, 93, 110–11, 113,
    124–26, 132
Bavinck, J. H. (Johan Herman,
    nephew of H. Bavinck), 23,
    115, 132–35
Bethlehem, 64
Bible, xv, xvi, 2–4, 30, 40, 45,
    52, 55, 62, 65–66, 81, 83,
    89, 91–92, 100, 102–3,
    109, 114, 116–17, 122, 137
bicycle, 121–23
Boniface, 116
Brock, Cory, 69, 110, 124
Byzantine Empire, the, 41

C

Caesar Augustus, 64
Cain, 11
Canaan, 12–13
Carson, D. A., 50–51

evangelicism (contemporary),
125
Eve, 8–9, 11, 14, 23
evil, 9–10, 15, 32, 101, 103

F
faith, 10, 20–21, 31, 41–44,
55–56, 68, 87, 94, 107,
116, 123–25, 127, 130–32,
134
Father (God as), 14, 16, 21,
61–63, 65–67, 75, 87, 116.
See also Trinity
Fleming, James, 5
folly, xv, 28, 32, 98, 103, 121
fool, 88–89
forms (cultural), 27–30, 35–36,
38, 53, 108–9, 111, 113–
15, 117, 120, 127, 130–31,
137
Frankfurt School, 35
fundamentalists, 43, 54

G
Galilee, 19
garden, the, 8–9, 11–13, 32.
See also Eden
Garo Christians (Bangladesh),
123
Germany, 116
Gethsemane, 75
Gettysburg Address, the, 37
Gilead (Robinson), 59
Gnosticism; Gnostics, 46, 50,
54

Godhead, the, 5, 65–66, 87.
See Trinity
*Gospel in a Pluralist Society,
The* (Newbigin), 97
Gotham, 76
grace (of God), 18, 22, 46,
51–58, 78, 82, 95, 128
Great Commandment, 73,
90–91

H
Haidt, Jonathan, 111
Henson, Jim, 1
history, 12, 24, 29, 38–40,
45, 47, 57, 69–70, 97,
100–105, 107–8, 115–16,
118–20, 125, 128, 138
Scripture as, 32, 38, 45,
100–105
Hobbes, Thomas, 2
Hogwarts, 76
hope, 21, 54, 93–94, 104, 107
human beings; humans
as creators of culture,
26–29, 31–32, 37, 47
direction of, 5–7
purpose of, 6–7, 9–10,
18–19, 33, 60, 67, 70,
74–77
structure of, 70–79
See also imagers

I
I Can Do It Myself (book
series), 1